ARTIFICIAL INTELLIGENCE FOR PROJECT MANAGERS

A Guide for Applying Artificial Intelligence to Projects through ChatGPT & Google Bard

PHILL AKINWALE, PMP, PMI-ACP, PSM, CSM

PUBLISHER

Praizion Media

Artificial Intelligence for Project Managers
Published by Praizion Media
P.O Box 22241, Mesa, AZ 85277
E-mail: info@praizion.com
www.praizion.com

Author
Phillip Akinwale, MSc, OPM3, PMP, PMI -RMP, PMI-SP, PMI-ACP, PSM, CSM

Copyright © 2023 Praizion Media

All rights reserved. No part of this publication may be reproduced, transmitted in any form or by any means including but not limited to electronic, recording, manual, mechanical, recording, photograph, photocopy, or stored in any retrieval system, without the prior written permission of the publisher.

ISBN 978-1-934579-28-2

The author and publisher make no warranties or representation that use of this publication will result in passing the PMP® exam or about the completeness and accuracy of the contents. The author and publisher accept no liability, losses or damages of any kind caused or alleged to be caused directly or indirectly by this publication.

PMI®, the PMI® logo, PMBOK® and PMP® are registered marks of the Project Management Institute, Inc. Project Management Institute, *A Guide to the Project Management Body of Knowledge (PMBOK® Guide)* Sixth Edition, Project Management Institute, Inc., 2017. Copyright and all rights reserved.

Printed in the United States of America

Table of Contents

INTRODUCTION 1

CHAPTER ONE: INTRODUCTION TO AI IN PROJECT MANAGEMENT 3

CHAPTER TWO: FOUNDATIONS OF PROJECT MANAGEMENT 12

CHAPTER THREE: AI AND PREDICTIVE PROJECT MANAGEMENT 24

CHAPTER FOUR: PROMPT ENGINEERING BASICS 33

CHAPTER FIVE: THE PATHFINDER PROMPT ENGINEERING SYSTEM FOR PROJECT MANAGERS 39

CHAPTER SIX: PREDICTIVE PROJECT MANAGEMENT PROMPTS 45

CHAPTER SEVEN: AGILE PROJECT MANAGEMENT AND AI INTEGRATION 96

CHAPTER EIGHT: AI IN HYBRID PROJECT MANAGEMENT 104

CHAPTER NINE: AI IN SCRUM PRACTICES 116

CHAPTER TEN: AI IN KANBAN PRACTICES 127

CHAPTER ELEVEN: DATA ANALYTICS AND AI IN PROJECT MANAGEMENT 135

CHAPTER TWELVE: AI IMPLEMENTATION AND ADOPTION STRATEGIES 145

CHAPTER THIRTEEN: AI FUTURE TRENDS IN PROJECT MANAGEMENT 150

CHAPTER FOURTEEN: CONCLUSION AND KEY TAKEAWAYS 155

Table of figures

Figure 1: Example of Project Charter Prompt in ChatGPT 47

Figure 2: Example of Project Charter Prompt in ChatGPT 50

Figure 3: Generated Output Example 51

Figure 4: How to copy a table from ChatGPT...52

Figure 5: Hybrid Responsibility Assignment Matrix from ChatGPT 113

Figure 6: Sample Team Data of Lines of Code Written Per Module 120

List of forms

Table 1: Simple Project Pathfinder Prompt Example 43

Table 2: Simple Project Charter Prompt Example 46

Table 3: Sample Formatted Project Charter from ChatGPT 57

Table 4: Formatted CRM Project Charter from ChatGPT 58

Table 5: Scope Management Plan from ChatGPT 61

Table 6: Requirements Management Plan from ChatGPT 62

Table 7: Requirements Traceability Matrix from ChatGPT 63

Table 8: Project Scope Statement from ChatGPT 64

Table 9: WBS from ChatGPT-Generated Data & Powerpoint 67

Table 10: Deliverable Acceptance Form from ChatGPT 68

Table 11: Assumption Log from ChatGPT..70

Table 12: Project Schedule From ChatGPT...71

Table 13: Project Budget From ChatGPT 72

Table 14: Earned Value Calculation Sheet from ChatGPT 73

Table 15: Quality Management Plan from ChatGPT 74

Table 16: Quality Report from ChatGPT 75

Table 17: Resource Management Plan from ChatGPT 76

Table 18: RACI Chart from ChatGPT...77

Table 19: Communications Management Plan from ChatGPT 78

Table 20: Risk Management Plan from ChatGPT 79

Table 21: Risk Register from ChatGPT 80

Table 22: Procurement Management Plan from ChatGPT 81

Table 23: Request for Proposal (RFP) from ChatGPT....................................82

Table 24: Contractual Agreement from ChatGPT 83

Table 25: Contractual Agreement from ChatGPT 84

Table 26: Stakeholder Engagement Plan from ChatGPT..............................85

Table 27: Work Performance Report from ChatGPT 86

Table 28: Issue Log from ChatGPT 87

Table 29: Risk Report from ChatGPT 88

Table 30: Lessons Learned Register from ChatGPT 89

Table 31: Project Management Plan Lite from ChatGPT 90

Table 32: Final Report from ChatGPT 91

Dedication

I dedicate this book to my kids, Jazzy, Joshy and Joy-Joy, my pride and joy and the future of AI! Thanks for all your support!

INTRODUCTION

> **"**
> *"I believe that artificial intelligence will be one of the most transformative technologies of our time, shaping industries, revolutionizing healthcare, and unlocking new possibilities for solving some of the world's toughest challenges."*
> *Bill Gates*

Phill, ever the beacon of sartorial elegance, stood at the front of the classroom wearing one of his trademark jazzy suits, an intricately patterned tie, and a shining watch from his vast collection. He cast his gaze across the unruly sea of faces in front of him. Some were eager, others were indifferent, and then there were the mischievous few who seemed bent on challenging Phill at every turn.

"Alright, class," he began, adjusting his tie slightly, *"Today we dive into the exciting fusion of artificial intelligence and project management. We'll begin by understanding AI. So, what is AI?"*

Several hands shot up. Among them was Sarah, the class president, known for her insightful questions. She crisply defined AI, outlining its history from Alan Turing to modern machine learning concepts.

Phill nodded approvingly, filling gaps and expanding on key ideas. Unexpectedly, class prankster Joey chimed in with a question about whether AI could predict the winning lottery numbers, leading to an enlightening discussion about the capabilities and limitations of AI.

Switching gears, Phill moved on to the basics of project management. He explained the process groups, knowledge areas, and the fundamental goal: delivering value. As expected, the class clown, Kevin, lightened the atmosphere by asking if project management could ensure his girlfriend's birthday party went off without a hitch. Phill smiled, skillfully weaving this into an explanation about the versatility of project management principles and how they could be applied to various scenarios, including personal events.

With the foundations set, Phill proceeded to discuss the intersection of AI and project management. He explained how AI could streamline processes, provide predictive analytics, and assist in decision-making. The serious students in the class, such as Sam and Mary, raised valid questions on AI's role in risk management and resource allocation. In contrast, the jokester group wondered if AI could replace project managers or, even better, substitute for them in boring meetings. Phill cleverly used these inquiries to highlight the tool-based role of AI and its potential to augment, rather than replace, human project managers.

CHAPTER ONE: INTRODUCTION TO AI IN PROJECT MANAGEMENT

"Minds are like parachutes; they only function when open."
Thomas Dewar

"Ahem! Okay, jokers and jesters and jolly ones alike," Phill began, adjusting his glistening Project Management Professional (PMP) lapel pin, which unabashedly announced his esteemed status to the world. His jovial tone settled even the most unruly in the room, a mixed bag of serious students and mischief-makers, all curious about the day's lesson in varying degrees.

"With that said," he added, snapping on the projector that came to life and cast a glow over his jazzy suit, "let us begin our journey into the world of Artificial Intelligence and its intersection with Project Management."

1.1 Understanding the Role of AI in Project Management

- Welcome to the exciting, sometimes mysterious, but always revolutionary world of Artificial Intelligence (AI) in Project Management.
- The role of AI here is similar to that quirky genius friend who seems to always have a solution before you've even fully grasped the problem. It's all about harnessing advanced algorithms, machine learning techniques, and a sprinkle of technological magic to take project management to a whole new level.

Artificial intelligence (AI) is rapidly transforming the way we work, and project management is no exception. AI-powered tools are already being used to automate tasks, improve decision-making, and optimize resources. As AI continues to develop, it is expected to have an even greater impact on project management.

There are many ways that AI can be used in project management. Here are a few examples:

- Automating tasks: AI can be used to automate repetitive tasks, such as data entry, scheduling, and reporting. This can free up project managers to focus on more strategic tasks.
- Improving decision-making: AI can be used to analyze data and identify patterns that would be difficult for humans to see. This can help project managers make better decisions about things like resource allocation, risk management, and scope definition.
- Optimizing resources: AI can be used to optimize resource allocation and scheduling. This can help projects run more efficiently and on time.

In the tangible terms, AI automates routine tasks, turning mountains of data into valuable insights and projecting likely future scenarios. Imagine, instead of spending hours sifting through data to track project performance or predict risks, an AI system does that for you, saving time and enhancing accuracy. That's the power of AI.

Amidst the academic discourse, prankster Joey interjected with a question, "So, can AI help me win a video game?" Chuckling, Phill used this as a teaching moment to journey into the practical applications and limitations of AI. "Pay close attention!" he began as the slide changed.

1.2 Benefits and Challenges of AI Adoption in Project Management

Like any good story, the journey of integrating AI into project management has its moments of triumph and trials. The benefits are compelling - increased efficiency, risk reduction, predictive capabilities, and a significant reduction in manual workload. Picture this: AI analyzing project data in real-time and identifying potential issues long before they become actual problems, giving project managers the foresight of an oracle.

There are many potential benefits to adopting AI in project management. These include:

- Increased efficiency: AI can automate tasks and improve decision-making, which can free up project managers to focus on more strategic tasks.

- Improved accuracy: AI can analyze data and identify patterns that would be difficult for humans to see. This can help project managers make better decisions.

- Increased visibility: AI can provide real-time insights into project progress. This can help project managers identify and address problems early on.

The challenges must also be acknowledged. AI implementation comes with cost considerations, requires appropriate skills, and a fundamental shift in traditional ways of managing projects. And there's the ever-present challenge of data privacy and security - just like you wouldn't want your personal diary read out loud, data handled by AI systems must be protected. Challenges to adopting AI in project management include:

- Cost: AI-powered tools can be expensive to purchase and implement.

- Technical expertise: AI requires a certain level of technical expertise to use effectively.

- Data quality: The accuracy of AI-powered tools depends on the quality of the data they are trained on.

- Ethical considerations: There are ethical considerations to using AI in project management, such as the potential for bias and discrimination.

The room filled with discussions of project management and managing triple constraints of scope, time, and cost. The class jester, Kevin, posed an amusing query, "So, can Project Management help me organize a rockin' party?" Phill, undeterred, adeptly connected the dots between project management principles and organizing successful events, emphasizing its universal applicability.

> **1.3 Ethical Considerations in AI-Driven Project Management**
>
> "We're stepping into deep waters here, but don't worry, we won't let you drown." Phill began, as the slide changed. AI-driven project management raises several ethical considerations. As AI systems make decisions, who is accountable for those decisions? What about the biases that AI might learn and perpetuate? How do we ensure transparency in AI's decision-making process? As project managers, we need to approach these questions not as barriers but as critical guideposts in our AI journey.

As AI becomes more widely used in project management, it is important to consider the ethical implications. Some of the ethical considerations that need to be addressed include:

- Bias: AI algorithms can be biased, which can lead to unfair or discriminatory decisions.

- Privacy: AI tools collect and analyze large amounts of data, which raises privacy concerns.

- Transparency: It is important to be transparent about how AI is being used in project management.

- Accountability: There needs to be a way to hold those who use AI accountable for their actions.

As the lesson drew to a close, Phill gave a brief overview of AI's impact on project management. He discussed case studies where AI drastically increased efficiency and predicted project outcomes with impressive accuracy. The more serious students in the room jotted down notes furiously, while the jesters pondered whether AI could make their homework disappear.

With a knowing smile, Phill set their minds at ease. "No, AI won't do your homework, but it will revolutionize the way we manage projects."

For the day's exercise, Phill tasked the class to reflect on traditional project management practices and imagine how AI could enhance them. As the students dispersed, Phill knew he had sparked their imaginations, and he looked forward to their responses, both the serious and the not-so-serious ones. After all, he mused, some of the best ideas can come from the most unlikely sources.

As the projector hummed to a stop, Phill assigned the day's exercise, asking the class to speculate on how AI might enhance traditional project management practices. Smiling at their lively chatter, Phill knew he had successfully planted the seeds of intrigue in their minds, paving the way for a captivating journey into the world of AI in Project Management.

1.4 Exercise: Reflecting on AI's Impact on Project Management

Alright, time to put on your thinking cap! Let's reflect on the impact of AI on project management.

Consider these questions:

1. What are the potential benefits of using AI in project management?

2. What processes in your current project management workflow could benefit from AI's ability to automate and analyze?

3. What challenges might you face in integrating AI into your project management practice? Think about resources, skills, and acceptance of the new technology.

4. Reflect on the ethical implications that could arise with AI adoption in your project. How would you navigate them?

5. How do you think AI will change the way project management is done in the future?

Remember, there's no right or wrong answer here. This exercise is about observing the landscape and plotting our course through it. In the upcoming chapters, we'll go deeper into these areas, providing you with tools and strategies to confidently navigate the world of AI in project management. So, are you ready to embark on this journey with us?

Chapter 1: Answers for Reflecting on AI's Impact on Project Management

1. The potential benefits of using AI in project management are numerous:

a. Improved efficiency: AI can automate repetitive tasks, such as data entry, scheduling, and documentation, allowing project managers to focus on more strategic and high-value activities.

b. Enhanced decision-making: AI can analyze vast amounts of data and provide insights and recommendations, helping project managers make informed decisions quickly and accurately.

c. Predictive analytics: AI algorithms can analyze historical project data, identify patterns, and make predictions about future outcomes, enabling proactive risk management and resource allocation.

d. Real-time monitoring: AI-powered tools can continuously monitor project progress, detect anomalies or delays, and alert project managers, enabling timely interventions and course corrections.

e. Resource optimization: AI can assist in optimizing resource allocation by analyzing historical data, identifying bottlenecks, and suggesting efficient resource utilization strategies, leading to cost savings and improved productivity.

2. Several processes in project management workflows can benefit from AI's automation and analysis capabilities:

a. Data analysis and reporting: AI can process large datasets, perform data analysis, and generate customized reports, saving significant time and effort.

b. Risk management: AI can analyze historical project data, identify risk factors, and provide early warning signals, enabling proactive risk mitigation strategies.

c. Task scheduling and optimization: AI algorithms can optimize task scheduling based on resource availability, dependencies, and constraints, minimizing project duration and maximizing efficiency.

d. Resource management: AI can analyze resource utilization patterns, identify potential overallocation or underutilization, and suggest optimal resource allocation strategies.

e. Communication and collaboration: AI-powered chatbots and virtual assistants can automate routine communication tasks, answer common queries, and facilitate collaboration among team members.

3. Integrating AI into project management practices may come with some challenges:

a. Resource allocation: Implementing AI in project management requires financial resources for acquiring AI tools and technologies, as well as the computational infrastructure to support them.

b. Skills and training: Project managers and team members may need training to effectively use AI tools and interpret the results. Upskilling or hiring personnel with AI expertise may be necessary.

c. Change management: Introducing AI may face resistance or skepticism from stakeholders who may fear job displacement or question the reliability of AI-generated insights. Change management efforts, including communication and education, are crucial to address these concerns.

d. Data quality and privacy: AI relies on quality data for accurate analysis and predictions. Ensuring data integrity, privacy, and compliance with data protection regulations is vital to maintain stakeholder trust.

4. **Reflecting on the ethical implications of AI adoption in project management is essential. Some considerations include:**

a. Bias and fairness: AI algorithms can inadvertently perpetuate biases present in the data used for training. It is crucial to ensure fairness and mitigate potential discrimination in decision-making processes.

b. Transparency and explainability: AI models often operate as black boxes, making it challenging to understand how decisions are reached. Striving for transparency and interpretability can help address concerns related to accountability and trust.

c. Privacy and data security: Project management involves handling sensitive and confidential data. Ensuring proper data protection measures, including data anonymization and access controls, is crucial to maintain privacy and prevent data breaches.

d. Accountability and human oversight: AI should augment human decision-making rather than replace it entirely. Maintaining human accountability and oversight is essential to address unforeseen circumstances and ensure ethical project management.

Navigating these ethical implications requires organizations to establish clear policies, standards, and governance frameworks, involving cross-functional teams, and seeking external expertise when necessary.

5. AI is likely to significantly change project management in the future:

a. Intelligent automation: AI will increasingly automate routine project management tasks, freeing up time for project managers to focus on strategic planning, stakeholder management, and value-added activities.

b. Advanced analytics: AI's ability to process and analyze vast amounts of data will enable more accurate predictions, smarter risk management, and optimized decision-making, leading to better project outcomes.

c. Enhanced collaboration: AI-powered collaboration tools, virtual assistants, and chatbots will facilitate seamless communication, knowledge sharing, and coordination among project team members, regardless of their physical location.

d. Agile and adaptive project management: AI can provide real-time insights, enabling project managers to adapt project plans and strategies quickly in response to changing circumstances, ensuring project success in dynamic environments.

e. Continuous improvement: AI's feedback loop and learning capabilities will enable project managers to continuously refine and improve their practices based on data-driven insights, fostering a culture of continuous improvement.

Overall, AI holds great promise for revolutionizing project management by streamlining processes, enabling data-driven decision-making, and augmenting human capabilities, leading to more efficient and successful project outcomes.

CHAPTER TWO: FOUNDATIONS OF PROJECT MANAGEMENT

> ❝
> *"Strong foundations breed successful projects."*

"Alright, class," Phill began, tapping his sparkling PMP lapel pin, the glint of his watch catching the morning light. "Today, we venture into the world of AI and predictive project management. Let's see what the future holds for us, shall we?"

The projector whirred to life, casting the first slide titled "Predictive Analytics in Project Management" on the whiteboard. Phill outlined the concept of predictive analytics, describing how it could be harnessed to forecast potential project outcomes. Kevin, never one to miss an opportunity for a wisecrack, quipped, "So, predictive analytics could tell me if I'll finally pass my math test?" Phill, ever patient, took this jest in stride and explained that while AI may not predict his math results, it could help educators identify areas of weakness in student performance.

Phill transitioned to the second slide, "Machine Learning for Predictive Project Management." He introduced the concept of machine learning and its application in analyzing past project data to predict future outcomes. As expected, serious students like Sam and Mary peppered Phill with questions about the nitty-gritty of machine learning algorithms. In contrast, the jesters in the class, including Joey, raised eyebrows and asked humorously if machine learning meant that their computers would start doing homework for them or teaching them advanced project management.

"Remember," Phill cautioned, with a hint of mirth in his eyes, "this is a Master's Degree program. I expect that you all remember the project management process groups and knowledge areas from our PMP Prep course last semester."

"Err..." Joey stammered, causing a ripple of laughter across the room.

"Err... what?" Phill shot back, a mischievous glint in his eyes. "You mean you want us to cover the basics AGAIN?"

"YESSS!" the class chorused, their faces lighting up with anticipation and mirth. Phill groaned dramatically, eliciting laughter from the students.

Shaking his head with a bemused smile, Phill navigated his way through the archive of past semester's slides and exhumed the once forgotten but now demanded deck on project management basics.

2.1 Overview of Project Management Process Groups

The first step in our journey into the world of project management is to understand its core – the process groups. These represent a logical grouping of project management processes to achieve specific project objectives. The five process groups as defined by the Project Management Institute (PMI) are: initiating, planning, executing, monitoring and controlling, and closing.

Remember, there's no right or wrong answer here. This exercise is about observing the landscape and plotting our course through it. In the upcoming chapters, we'll go deeper into these areas, providing you with tools and strategies to confidently navigate the world of AI in project management. So, are you ready to embark on this journey with us?

- Initiating: This process group involves defining the project, its goals, and its scope. In the initiating process group, the project's objectives and deliverables are defined, and the project's feasibility is evaluated. This stage serves as the springboard for the project, outlining its value and purpose.

- Planning: This process group involves creating a detailed plan for how the project will be executed. The planning process group is where detailed planning of the project occurs, covering all aspects from scope, cost, quality, procurement, to risk and communication among others. This is the blueprint of your project, charting out the how, who, when, and where.

- Executing: This process group involves carrying out the project plan. Executing is where the plan is put into action to produce the project's deliverables. This process group is all about resource allocation, task delegation, and leading the team to accomplish the set objectives.

- Monitoring and Controlling: This process group involves tracking the project's progress and making adjustments as needed. The monitoring and controlling process group involves tracking the project's progress against the planned objectives and making adjustments as needed. This ongoing process ensures that the project stays on track and within the set boundaries.

- Closing: This process group involves finalizing the project and delivering the product or service.

  Finalizing all activities, documenting lessons learned, and formally closing the project. This is an important step to reflect on the achievements and take away key learnings for future projects.

Phill continued to the knowledge area slides next.

2.2 Introduction to Project Management Knowledge Areas

Knowledge areas in project management refer to the ten areas of expertise needed to successfully manage a project. These include: Integration, Scope, Schedule, Cost, Quality, Resource, Communication, Risk, Procurement, and Stakeholder Management. Each of these areas intertwine and interact with the five process groups, creating a comprehensive matrix of activities that guide the project from initiation to closure.

Project management knowledge areas are the different areas of expertise that are needed to successfully manage a project. These knowledge areas include:

- Project Scope Management: This knowledge area involves defining the project scope and ensuring that the project stays on track.

- Project Schedule Management: This knowledge area involves creating and managing the project schedule.

- Project Cost Management: This knowledge area involves estimating, budgeting, and managing the project costs.

- Project Quality Management: This knowledge area involves ensuring that the project meets the required quality standards.

- Project Resource Management: This knowledge area involves acquiring resources, developing, and managing the project team. This includes both tangible resources, such as people, equipment, and materials, and intangible resources, such as time and information.

- Project Communication Management: This knowledge area involves ensuring that the project communicates effectively with its stakeholders.

- Project Risk Management: This knowledge area involves identifying, assessing, and mitigating project risks.

- Project Procurement Management: This knowledge area involves acquiring the goods and services needed to complete the project.

- Project Stakeholder Management involves identifying, analyzing, and managing the people who have an interest in the project. This includes both internal stakeholders, such as the project team and the project sponsor, and external stakeholders, such as customers, suppliers, and regulators.

Just as Phill seemed to be making headway with the process groups and knowledge areas, a shrill voice cut through the hum of the projector.

"HOW ABOUT AGILE?"

The word echoed in the room, leaving a resonating silence behind. Phill blinked at his class, his expression a mix of surprise and exasperation.

"Agile?" He echoed, his eyebrows arching in disbelief. "Are you kidding me right now? You want me to go over Agile, which we covered last year too?"

"YESSS!" The response was almost deafening.

Phill shook his head in good-natured resignation and, amidst chuckles and guffaws, trawled through the virtual cobwebs of his archives to unearth the slides from the Agile module. The dusty title slide popped up on the screen, 'Agile Project Management: Embracing Change.'

With a resigned sigh and a playful glint in his eyes, Phill began his impromptu Agile refresher. "Agile," he started, "is not a methodology, framework, or a set of practices. It's far more than that. It's a mindset, a philosophy, a disposition towards the ever-changing world around us."

As the first slide titled "Introduction to Agile Project Management" flickered onto the screen, Phill could see curiosity piquing in his students' eyes. He guided them back through the tenets of the Agile Manifesto, emphasizing the value of individuals and interactions, working products, customer collaboration, and responding to change. The room fell silent, save for the occasional note-taking scribble and the hum of the projector, as Phill breathed life back into the Agile principles.

2.3 Introduction to Agile

Agile, a term widely used (often incorrectly) in the realm of project management, often gets misunderstood. Agile is neither a methodology nor a specific framework; it is, in essence, a mindset. This mindset is embodied in the Agile Manifesto, a revolutionary document crafted by 17 professionals I consider to be pioneers in 2001. It presented a fresh perspective on tackling product development and complex problems, prioritizing individuals and interactions over processes and tools, working products over comprehensive documentation, customer collaboration over contract negotiation, and responding to change over following a plan.

He described the Agile mindset; adaptability, customer focus, and iterative progress, blending seamlessly with the previous detour. Mischief-maker Joey perked up, wondering aloud if "going Agile" meant fewer assignments. Phill, rising to the challenge, quipped back that perhaps it meant iterative, frequent assignments instead, much to the amusement of the class.

At that moment, the class was a testament to the Agile philosophy itself – adaptable, responsive, and ever ready to embrace change, even when it came in the form of an unexpected lesson.
The projector beamed on to the next section.

> **2.4 Aligning AI with Project Management Frameworks**
>
> There are many different project management frameworks that can be used to guide the project management process. These frameworks typically provide a set of best practices and tools that can be used to improve the effectiveness of project management.

AI can be aligned with project management frameworks in a number of ways. For example, AI can be used to automate tasks, improve decision-making, and optimize resources. AI can also be used to collect and analyze data, which can be used to improve the effectiveness of project management frameworks.

Artificial Intelligence (AI) is not just a buzzword in project management; it's a strategic tool that can enhance efficiency and effectiveness. To align AI with project management, we must first identify the areas where AI can add value. These include data analysis, risk assessment, resource allocation, and task automation among others.

Machine learning algorithms can sift through large volumes of data and derive insights faster than any human could, making them ideal for predictive analysis and decision-making. Similarly, AI can improve risk management by identifying patterns and trends that could signal potential issues.

AI-powered chatbots can streamline communication, ensuring that all team members have access to real-time information and updates. Furthermore, AI can help optimize resource allocation, using algorithms to match tasks with the most suitable resources, improving efficiency and productivity.

Before wrapping up, Phill assigned an exciting exercise to the class, prompting them to use a hypothetical project dataset to predict outcomes using basic machine learning algorithms.

2.5 Exercise: Identifying AI Opportunities in Project Management Process Groups

As we go into the intersections of AI and project management, let's pause and identify some potential AI opportunities within the five project management process groups. Consider the following questions:

1. How can AI support the initiating process group? Consider areas such as feasibility studies and setting objectives.
2. In the planning stage, where can AI assist in refining the project plan and mitigating risks?
3. How might AI enhance the execution of a project, especially in terms of resource allocation and quality control?
4. In what ways can AI aid in monitoring and controlling a project? Think about predictive analysis and real-time updates.
5. Finally, how can AI facilitate the closing process group, particularly in the aspects of lessons learned and project documentation?
6. How can AI aid the project manager in each knowledge area?
7. How can AI enhance Agile practices, principles and frameworks?

As we explore these questions, we start to see the transformative potential of AI in project management. In the chapters to come, we will dive deeper into each of these aspects, building a comprehensive understanding of AI's role and possibilities in project management.

In addition to the traditional project management concepts, AI is also becoming an increasingly important part of project management. By aligning AI with project management frameworks, project managers can use AI to automate tasks, improve decision-making, and optimize resources. This can help project managers to improve the efficiency and effectiveness of their projects.

As the projector hummed to a stop and the class disbanded, Phill sat back, content with the day's proceedings. The blend of seriousness and silliness had, once again, led to a dynamic, engaging, and unforgettable session.

Chapter 2: Answers

1. AI can support the initiating process group in the following ways:

    - Feasibility studies: AI can analyze historical project data, market trends, and other relevant information to provide insights into the feasibility of a project. It can identify potential risks, estimate costs, and predict project outcomes, helping stakeholders make informed decisions.

    - Setting objectives: AI can assist in defining clear and measurable project objectives by analyzing past project performance, industry benchmarks, and best practices. It can provide recommendations for setting realistic goals and aligning them with organizational strategies.

    - Developing a project charter template specific to your organization or industry.

2. In the planning stage, AI can assist in refining the project plan and mitigating risks:

    - Project plan optimization: AI algorithms can analyze project requirements, constraints, and dependencies to optimize project schedules and resource allocation. It can identify bottlenecks, suggest alternative approaches, and help in creating an efficient project plan.

    - Risk identification and analysis: AI can analyze historical project data, external factors, and industry trends to identify potential risks. It can help project managers assess risk probabilities, prioritize risks, and develop effective mitigation strategies based on data-driven insights.

3. AI can enhance the execution of a project, especially in terms of resource allocation and quality control:

    - Resource allocation: AI algorithms can analyze resource availability, skill sets, and project requirements to suggest optimal resource allocation strategies. It can help project managers match resources with tasks, optimize workloads, and minimize resource conflicts.

- Quality control: AI-powered tools can analyze project deliverables, data, and performance metrics to identify deviations from quality standards. It can detect anomalies, recommend corrective actions, and ensure adherence to quality requirements.

4. AI can aid in monitoring and controlling a project through predictive analysis and real-time updates:

- Predictive analysis: AI algorithms can analyze project data, performance metrics, and historical patterns to make predictions about future outcomes. It can help project managers anticipate potential risks, assess project progress, and take proactive measures to address issues before they escalate.

- Real-time updates: AI-powered monitoring systems can continuously collect and analyze real-time project data, providing project managers with up-to-date information on project status, resource utilization, and key performance indicators. It can generate alerts and notifications for timely interventions and decision-making.

5. AI can facilitate the closing process group, particularly in the aspects of lessons learned and project documentation:

- Lessons learned: AI can analyze project data, documentation, and feedback from team members to identify lessons learned throughout the project lifecycle. It can extract valuable insights, patterns, and best practices, enabling project managers to capture and document knowledge for future projects.

- Project documentation: AI can assist in automating the documentation process by analyzing project data, milestones, and deliverables. It can generate standardized reports, project summaries, and documentation templates, reducing manual effort and improving documentation accuracy.

6. AI can aid the project manager in each knowledge area:

- Integration management: AI can assist in integrating project processes, data, and documentation, ensuring seamless collaboration and communication across various project management areas.

- Scope management: AI can help in defining project scope, analyzing requirements, and identifying scope changes or deviations through data analysis and automated monitoring.

- Time management: AI can optimize project schedules, task dependencies, and critical path analysis to ensure efficient time management and timely project completion.

- Cost management: AI can assist in cost estimation, budget allocation, and monitoring of project expenditures by analyzing historical data, resource utilization, and cost trends.

- Quality management: AI can analyze project deliverables, performance metrics, and customer feedback to ensure adherence to quality standards and drive continuous improvement.

- Human resource management: AI can support resource allocation, skill matching, and performance evaluation to optimize the utilization of human resources and enhance team productivity.

- Communications management: AI-powered chatbots and virtual assistants can automate routine communication tasks, facilitate collaboration, and provide stakeholders with timely project updates and information.

- Risk management: AI can assist in risk identification, analysis, and response planning by analyzing historical data, market trends, and project parameters to help project managers mitigate risks effectively.

- Procurement management: AI can automate procurement processes, analyze supplier data, and optimize procurement strategies to ensure cost-effectiveness and minimize procurement risks.

7. AI can enhance Agile practices, principles, and frameworks:

- Agile planning and estimation: AI can assist in backlog prioritization, story point estimation, and sprint planning by analyzing historical data, team velocity, and stakeholder priorities. It can provide insights and recommendations to improve planning accuracy and optimize resource allocation.

- Continuous integration and delivery: AI-powered tools can automate code reviews, identify bugs, and support continuous integration and delivery practices in software development projects. It can enhance efficiency, reduce errors, and accelerate the software development life cycle.

- Team collaboration and communication: AI-powered collaboration tools, virtual assistants, and chatbots can facilitate real-time communication, knowledge sharing, and collaboration among Agile team members, ensuring seamless coordination and information flow.

- Agile metrics and performance tracking: AI can analyze Agile project metrics, team performance, and customer feedback to provide insights into project progress, team dynamics, and areas for improvement. It can help Agile teams measure and track performance against Agile principles and identify opportunities for continuous improvement.

Overall, AI has the potential to augment project management processes and enable project managers to make more informed decisions, optimize resource utilization, mitigate risks, and improve project outcomes across all project management process groups and knowledge areas.

CHAPTER THREE: AI AND PREDICTIVE PROJECT MANAGEMENT

> ## "
> *"Needs must be assessed before forging ahead on a project full-force!"*

In the aftermath of the Agile refresher, the room buzzed with energy, and Phill's PMP lapel pin shone even brighter, if that was possible. Clearing his throat, he prepared to navigate the class back on track - towards the day's original lesson plan, AI and Predictive Project Management.

"Alright, back to business everyone," Phill began, revealing the first slide titled "Introduction to Predictive Project Management." He started with the basics, explaining the core aspects of predictive project management, its reliance on detailed planning and the crucial role data played in its successful execution.

The slide displayed the information as shown:

> **3.1 Recap on Predictive Project Management and AI**
>
> There are many different AI techniques that can be used for predictive project management. These techniques include:
>
> - Machine learning: Machine learning can be used to analyze historical data and identify patterns that can be used to predict future outcomes.
>
> - Natural language processing: Natural language processing can be used to analyze text data, such as emails, meeting notes, and project documentation. This can help project managers to identify risks and opportunities that may not be obvious from other data sources.
>
> - Data visualization: Data visualization can be used to present data in a way that is easy to understand and interpret. This can help project managers to make better decisions about how to plan and execute the project.

Predictive project management involves using historical data, statistical analysis, and mathematical models to forecast project outcomes, identify potential risks, and make informed decisions. The PMBOK® Guide Sixth and Seventh Editions are good predictive project management references.

AI plays a significant role in enhancing predictive project management by leveraging its capabilities in data analysis, pattern recognition, and machine learning. With AI, project managers can go beyond traditional project planning and scheduling methods and gain valuable insights for more accurate predictions and proactive decision-making.

"Now, before we move forward," Phill said, eyeing his rambunctious class, "Does anyone have any jokes or questions about predictive project management, or should I say, 'can it predict when our next pop quiz will be'?" He mimicked with a grin, earning a round of laughter.

With the class firmly re-routed, Phill moved to the next section, "AI-Enhanced Project Planning and Scheduling." He talked about how AI could help in predicting project timelines, budgets, and resources based on historical data. Kevin, ever the class comic, jokingly inquired if it meant he could finally predict when his assignments would get done. Phill, with his usual grace, took the joke and spun it into a lesson, explaining that yes, theoretically, AI could predict task completion based on past performance data.

The slide displayed the information as shown:

3.2 AI-Enhanced Project Planning and Scheduling

AI can be used to enhance project planning and scheduling in a number of ways. For example, AI can be used to:

- Automate the creation of project plans: AI can be used to analyze historical data and identify the best practices for creating project plans. This can save project managers a significant amount of time and effort.

- Identify potential risks and opportunities: AI can be used to analyze data and identify potential risks and opportunities that may not be obvious to project managers. This can help project managers to make better decisions about how to mitigate risks and take advantage of opportunities.

- Optimize the project schedule: AI can be used to optimize the project schedule by taking into account factors such as resource availability, task dependencies, and risk. This can help project managers to ensure that the project is completed on time and within budget.

AI brings significant enhancements to project planning and scheduling processes. By analyzing historical project data, AI algorithms can identify patterns, dependencies, and critical paths, helping project managers create more realistic and optimized project plans.

AI can consider multiple variables, such as resource availability, task dependencies, and constraints, to generate schedules that maximize efficiency and minimize project duration. It can also simulate various scenarios and provide recommendations to handle schedule changes and uncertainties.

AI-powered planning and scheduling tools enable project managers to proactively address potential delays, optimize resource allocation, and improve overall project performance.

"AI-Driven Resource Optimization" was next on the agenda. Phill outlined how AI could assist in allocating resources efficiently and effectively, ensuring optimal productivity. Even Joey chimed in, asking if AI could help optimize his weekend plans. Phill, while smiling at the jest, retorted that it might not be too far off if Joey recorded his historical data accurately.

Moving swiftly on, Phill went on to the content slide:

3.3 AI-Driven Resource Optimization

AI can also be used to optimize resource allocation in a project. For example, AI can be used to:

- Identify the most efficient use of resources: AI can be used to analyze data and identify the most efficient way to allocate resources to tasks. This can help project managers to save money and improve the efficiency of the project.
- Predict resource availability: AI can be used to predict resource availability in the future. This can help project managers to make better decisions about how to allocate resources to tasks.

Rebalance resource allocation: AI can be used to rebalance resource allocation in the event of unexpected events. This can help project managers to ensure that the project remains on track.

Resource optimization is a critical aspect of project management, and AI can greatly assist in this area. AI algorithms can analyze historical resource utilization data, identify patterns and trends, and provide recommendations for optimal resource allocation.

By considering factors such as resource availability, skill sets, and task requirements, AI can suggest the most efficient allocation strategies. It can also identify potential bottlenecks, balance workloads, and help project managers make data-driven decisions to maximize resource utilization and minimize costs.

AI-driven resource optimization enables project teams to achieve better project outcomes, improve productivity, and avoid resource conflicts.

Finally, Phill unveiled the exercise for the day: Applying AI Techniques to Predictive Project Management. The assignment was met with the usual mixed reactions, groans from the jesters, and thoughtful nods from the more serious students. Phill beamed the slide up on the screen:

3.4 Exercise: Applying AI Techniques to Predictive Project Management

1. How can you leverage AI algorithms and data analysis to improve your project's predictive capabilities?
2. What historical project data would you need to collect and analyze to train an AI model for predicting project outcomes?
3. What specific risks or challenges could AI help you identify and mitigate in your project?
4. How would you incorporate real-time monitoring and alerts into your project management approach using AI?
5. Which project resources do you think would benefit the most from AI-driven optimization? How would you determine the optimal allocation of those resources?
6. How can AI assist in decision-making processes within your project? What types of decisions would you trust an AI algorithm to support?
7. What steps would you take to ensure the ethical use of AI in predictive project management? How would you address concerns related to bias, transparency, and privacy?
8. What potential limitations or risks do you foresee in implementing AI techniques in your project management approach, and how would you mitigate them?
9. How would you communicate the benefits and value of integrating AI into your predictive project management practices to stakeholders and team members?
10. How could you measure and evaluate the effectiveness of AI techniques in improving your project's predictability and performance?
11. Use AI to generate a project charter and stakeholder register.

As the projector flickered off, Phill was content. The class had navigated unexpected detours but ultimately arrived at the day's intended destination. After all, the journey, filled with laughter and learning, was what made his job worthwhile.

Chapter 3 Answers: Applying AI Techniques to Predictive Project Management

1. How can you leverage AI algorithms and data analysis to improve your project's predictive capabilities? By leveraging AI algorithms and data analysis, we can analyze historical project data to identify patterns and trends that contribute to project outcomes. This analysis can help us develop predictive models that can forecast project timelines, resource requirements, and potential risks. AI algorithms can process large amounts of data, identify complex relationships, and provide insights that can enhance the accuracy and reliability of our project predictions.

2. What historical project data would you need to collect and analyze to train an AI model for predicting project outcomes? To train an AI model for predicting project outcomes, we would need historical data such as project schedules, resource allocation information, task completion times, risk logs, and project performance metrics. Additionally, data on external factors that may impact project outcomes, such as market conditions or regulatory changes, could be valuable. The more comprehensive and diverse the historical data, the better our AI model can learn and make accurate predictions.

3. What specific risks or challenges could AI help you identify and mitigate in your project? AI can help identify and mitigate various risks in projects. For example, by analyzing historical data and external factors, AI algorithms can identify risks related to resource constraints, budget overruns, schedule delays, and scope changes. AI can also help in risk prioritization, recommending mitigation strategies, and providing insights for contingency planning. By identifying risks early on and providing data-driven insights, AI can enable proactive risk management and improve the project's overall resilience.

4. How would you incorporate real-time monitoring and alerts into your project management approach using AI? To incorporate real-time monitoring and alerts using AI, we would implement AI-powered monitoring systems that continuously collect and analyze project data in real-time. By setting thresholds and predefined rules, AI algorithms can generate alerts and notifications when deviations occur or when specific conditions are met. These alerts can be

sent to project managers, stakeholders, or relevant team members, enabling timely interventions, issue resolution, and proactive decision-making based on up-to-date information.

5. Which project resources do you think would benefit the most from AI-driven optimization? How would you determine the optimal allocation of those resources? Resource optimization can greatly benefit from AI-driven approaches. Key project resources such as human resources, equipment, and materials can be optimized using AI algorithms. The optimal allocation of resources can be determined by analyzing historical resource utilization data, project requirements, skill sets, and dependencies. AI algorithms can suggest resource allocation strategies that minimize conflicts, maximize utilization, and consider factors such as resource availability, expertise, and project priorities. By leveraging AI-driven optimization, we can ensure efficient resource allocation and avoid bottlenecks or underutilization.

6. How can AI assist in decision-making processes within your project? What types of decisions would you trust an AI algorithm to support? AI can assist in decision-making processes by providing data-driven insights, recommendations, and scenario analysis. AI algorithms can process vast amounts of data, analyze patterns, and identify correlations that humans may overlook. This can support decisions related to project planning, risk assessment, resource allocation, and schedule optimization. While AI algorithms can provide valuable recommendations, it's important to exercise human judgment and consider the limitations of AI. Critical decisions that involve ethical considerations, stakeholder relationships, or strategic direction should be made with human oversight and accountability.

7. What steps would you take to ensure the ethical use of AI in predictive project management? How would you address concerns related to bias, transparency, and privacy? To ensure the ethical use of AI in predictive project management, we would take several steps. First, we would ensure that the data used to train AI models is representative, unbiased, and diverse. We would carefully select and preprocess data to minimize biases and address potential ethical

concerns. Transparency would be promoted by documenting the AI algorithms, data sources, and processing methods used. We would implement privacy safeguards to protect sensitive project data and comply with relevant regulations. Regular audits and assessments would be conducted to identify and rectify any biases or ethical issues that may arise during AI usage.

8. What potential limitations or risks do you foresee in implementing AI techniques in your project management approach, and how would you mitigate them? Implementing AI techniques in project management may present challenges and risks. Some potential limitations include the need for high-quality and diverse historical data, the requirement for skilled personnel to develop and interpret AI models, and the possibility of overreliance on AI-generated insights. To mitigate these risks, we would invest in data collection and quality assurance processes, provide training for project managers to understand AI outputs, and foster a culture of human oversight and critical thinking. Regular monitoring, validation, and calibration of AI models would be performed to ensure their accuracy and reliability.

9. How would you communicate the benefits and value of integrating AI into your predictive project management practices to stakeholders and team members? To communicate the benefits and value of integrating AI into predictive project management practices, we would highlight how AI can enhance project outcomes, improve decision-making, and mitigate risks. We would emphasize the efficiency gains, accuracy improvements, and resource optimization that AI can bring. Demonstrating successful case studies and sharing examples of AI-enabled insights and predictions would help stakeholders and team members understand the tangible benefits. Clear communication about how AI complements human expertise and judgment would be crucial to address any concerns or misconceptions.

10. How could you measure and evaluate the effectiveness of AI techniques in improving your project's predictability and performance? To measure and evaluate the effectiveness of AI techniques, we would establish key performance indicators (KPIs) related to project predictability and performance. These could include metrics such as project completion time,

resource utilization rates, risk identification and mitigation effectiveness, and accuracy of project predictions. By comparing project outcomes before and after implementing AI techniques, we can assess the impact of AI on these KPIs. Regular feedback from project stakeholders and team members can also provide insights into the perceived value and effectiveness of AI techniques in improving project outcomes.

CHAPTER FOUR: PROMPT ENGINEERING BASICS

"

""Prompt engineering can be seen as the literacy skill set that tomorrow's project managers will need to master.""

Following the exercise announcement, the hum of discussion began to fill the room. But Phill, ever the seasoned navigator of educational ebb and flow, knew it was time to steer the class towards uncharted territories. His eyes twinkled with anticipation as he revealed the title of the next section: "Introduction to Prompt Engineering Basics."

"Alright, folks!" Phill said, a broad grin spreading across his face, mirroring his excitement. "It's time to shift gears a bit and explore an area where AI shines exceptionally - prompt engineering."

His proclamation was met with a few blank faces, some intrigued looks, and Kevin's raised hand. "So, like, is that engineering homework prompts, so we don't have to do them?" he quipped, earning a wave of laughter.

With a chuckle, Phill responded, "If only it were that easy, Kevin! But no, prompt engineering is a fascinating part of AI development. It's about designing and refining prompts or instructions for AI to follow, particularly language models like the one we've been discussing."

Phill moved to the projector to bring up a simple illustration of a language model receiving a text prompt and generating a continuation. "AI language models learn from vast amounts of text data," he explained, "and prompt engineering is about providing the right nudge, the right direction for these models to generate desired responses."

The projector beamed a video walking through the intricacies of prompt engineering with the steady smooth voice of Peter Baker, the narrator:

> **4.1 Prompt Engineering Basics**
>
> As AI continues to advance and integrate into various aspects of our lives, it becomes essential to understand how prompts shape the behavior and decision-making of AI models. The prompts we provide act as instructions that guide the AI in generating the desired outputs. Therefore, the quality and specificity of the prompts directly impact the accuracy and relevance of the AI's responses.
>
> Prompt engineering is particularly crucial in the realm of natural language processing (NLP), where AI models are designed to understand and generate human-like language. By carefully designing prompts, we can ensure that the AI accurately comprehends the task at hand and generates responses that meet our expectations.

The importance of precise and robust prompts cannot be overstated. They serve as the foundation for effective communication with AI models, enabling us to extract the desired information or achieve specific tasks. When prompts are vague or poorly constructed, the AI may struggle to understand our intentions, resulting in inaccurate or irrelevant outputs.

4.2 Good vs. Bad Prompts

Consider a scenario where we want to translate a sentence to French. A poor prompt would be "Translate this sentence to French," as it lacks the necessary information. In contrast, a good prompt would be "Please translate the following sentence into French: 'I would like to order a coffee and a croissant.'" The latter prompt provides clear instructions and specific details, ensuring that the AI understands our request accurately.

Another example can be seen in a writing task. Asking the AI to "Write a short story" is vague and leaves room for interpretation. However, a more effective prompt would be "Write a 500-word short story that includes the following three elements: a red balloon, a deserted beach, and a mysterious stranger." By providing specific criteria, we guide the AI's creativity and ensure that the resulting story aligns with our intentions.

4.3 Explicit Prompts

Explicit prompts are commands or instructions that precisely articulate the task the model needs to perform. These prompts are characterized by clarity and specificity. They leave little to no room for ambiguity, as they detail the nature of the output the user expects.

An explicit prompt can be as simple as "Write a poem about a flower." Here, the user is expressly asking the language model to compose a poem, and the subject of the poem is clearly defined as a flower. The instruction is direct and unambiguous.

Explicit prompts can also be more complex, requiring the model to perform tasks involving a series of steps. For example, consider the explicit prompt, "Read the following text and summarize it in three sentences." The model is clearly instructed first to read or process a given text and then to produce a summary condensed into three sentences.

The effectiveness of explicit prompts lies in their precision. They provide a roadmap that the model can follow, enabling it to generate responses that align closely with the user's intent.

Explicit prompts also enhance the model's ability to handle tasks that require a structured response. In the context of a writing task, for instance, an explicit prompt like "Write an essay discussing the causes and effects of climate change" will guide the model to produce an essay that not only addresses the specific topic (climate change) but also covers the specific aspects of the topic (causes and effects).

Explicit prompts can be particularly useful in educational and professional applications. They can guide language models to generate specific and structured responses or content, such as essays, reports, lesson plans, business plans, code snippets, and more.

4.4 Implicit Prompts

Implicit prompts, on the other hand, convey the task to the language model in a less direct manner. These prompts are often more open-ended, leaving room for interpretation. The user is still guiding the model's response but in a less restrictive way, allowing the model to generate a broader range of responses.

Take the implicit prompt "Describe a flower," for example. This instruction doesn't specify the format or structure of the response. The model could choose to describe a flower scientifically, focusing on its biological characteristics. Alternatively, it could take a more poetic approach, describing the flower's beauty and fragrance. The prompt guides the model to provide information about a flower, but the nature and style of the response are left open-ended.

Implicit prompts stimulate the model to exhibit its creative and generative capabilities. For instance, if a user provides the prompt, "It was a dark and stormy night," the model might generate a suspenseful short story, an atmospheric poem, or a descriptive paragraph. The ambiguity allows for a multitude of possible responses, each displaying the model's ability to create original content based on the given trigger.

Implicit prompts also allow users to explore the model's ability to adapt to context and extrapolate from incomplete information. For example, if a user provides the prompt, "As the sun set," the model could continue the narrative in a variety of ways, depending on the context provided or inferred. Implicit prompts can prove useful in a range of scenarios, particularly those that benefit from creativity, variety, and exploration. They can help generate diverse narrative content, ideate for brainstorming sessions, or even assist in creating various forms of artistic expression, such as stories, poems, and scripts.

4.5 Prompts in Image Generation

In the same vein, prompt engineering plays a crucial role in image generation tasks. When requesting an image from an AI, it is essential to provide clear and precise prompts regarding the desired style, subject matter, and other visual characteristics.

For example, instead of simply asking the AI to "Generate an image of a cat," a better prompt would be "Please generate an image of a white Persian cat sitting on a windowsill, looking out at the moonlit city skyline." This level of detail ensures that the AI produces an image that matches our specific requirements.

4.6 Good Prompt Structure

Prompt engineering involves designing prompts that are concise, focused, and accurately convey the intended meaning. It requires careful consideration of the context in which the prompts will be used and tailoring them accordingly. For instance, a prompt designed for a chatbot would differ from one designed for language translation.

Active verbs can bring more energy and urgency to prompts, making them more effective in guiding the AI's decision-making. Additionally, incorporating relevant domain-specific knowledge into prompts helps align the AI's responses with the desired outcomes. It is also crucial to consider the audience for whom the prompts are intended, as this influences the language and tone used in the prompts.

4.7 The Importance of Good Prompts

Prompt engineering is a critical aspect of developing AI models that can generate high-quality outputs meeting the needs and expectations of users. By mastering the art of prompt engineering, we can leverage the power of AI to automate tasks, enhance decision-making processes, and streamline various aspects of our lives.

To ensure the effectiveness of prompts, it is essential to test them with real users and gather feedback on their clarity and effectiveness. Continuous iteration and improvement of prompt design based on user feedback and performance metrics lead to more effective AI models.

4.8 Three Rules for Effective Prompts

1. Be clear and concise. The Large Language Model (LLM) should be able to understand what you are asking for without having to guess.
2. Provide enough context. The more context you provide, the better the LLM will be able to generate a response.
3. Be specific. The more specific you are, the more likely the LLM is to generate a response that is relevant to your needs.

As Phill went deeper into the topic, discussing the importance of precision in prompt formulation, contextual cues, and tweaking prompts for better results, the class was unusually silent. Even the jesters seemed to be in deep thought, contemplating this newly introduced AI concept.

Phill could see the gears turning in his students' minds. He was once again reminded why he loved his job so much - the thrill of introducing new concepts, the challenge of simplifying complex ideas, and the reward of watching understanding dawn on his students' faces. All these made every unruly day worth it.

CHAPTER FIVE: THE PATHFINDER PROMPT ENGINEERING SYSTEM FOR PROJECT MANAGERS

"Success is not a matter of chance, it's a path well-charted. The Pathfinder system reveals the signposts that guide us to a triumphant project manager-AI collaboration!"

Introduction to Prompt Engineering

In the advent of modern technology, artificial intelligence (AI) tools, like ChatGPT, offer unprecedented levels of assistance in project management. However, the effectiveness of these AI tools hinges on the degree of detail specified in the prompts given. In the realm of project management, the development of a well-crafted prompt is crucial for creating comprehensive project management documents and plans.

This chapter aims to educate the reader about the meticulous process of creating comprehensive prompts for project management documents, and how to make the most out of AI capabilities. We explore the significance of including every single aspect of detail in a prompt and provides guidelines for structuring prompts to extract the desired information effectively. Furthermore, we will study the process of querying intelligent tools like ChatGPT to obtain optimal outputs.

5.1: The Importance of Detailed Prompts

5.1.1 Absorbing Detailed Information: When engaging with AI, there's no such thing as too much detail. Whether it's a project management document, plan, or report, each task must be outlined meticulously to ensure accurate and efficient output. The tool can process vast amounts of text, so holding back on details would mean losing out on the full potential of the AI.

5.1.2 Utilizing Tables and Rows: A useful strategy to lay down your expectations is to use tables, rows of text, or columns. This enables you to categorize your information systematically, fostering enhanced comprehension for the AI, and consequently, generating outputs that align with your requirements.

Understand that ChatGPT can assimilate paragraphs and pages of text, it is essential not to withhold any pertinent details. By listing out all the required fields, regardless of their quantity, project managers can ensure that the prompt encapsulates the complete scope of the project. You can copy entire spreadsheets and paste them into the tool. It will understand it all. To organize the information within the prompt, project managers can make use of tables, rows of text, or even columns. These formatting techniques enable a clear and structured representation of various aspects of the project, facilitating better comprehension and analysis.

5.2: The Project Pathfinder Prompt System

One way to ensure the completeness of your prompts is to incorporate the '5W' principle, widely recognized in journalism and research: Who, What, When, Where, Why, How and "Other". I call this the Project Pathfinder Prompt System.

5.2.1 **What**: Clearly defining the objective of the project and the specific deliverables expected from the system is imperative. Including a detailed description of what needs to be accomplished helps set a clear direction for both the project manager and the intelligent tool.

Detail the nature of the project management document you're working on and articulate the outcome you anticipate from the AI.

5.2.2 **When**: If there are time constraints or specific deadlines associated with the project or its components, it is essential to include them in the prompt. Mentioning dates or time frames allows the intelligent tool to consider temporal aspects while generating outputs.

Specify if there's a deadline or a schedule the AI needs to consider when preparing the document.

5.2.3 **Where**: Project management often involves physical or geographical considerations. If location plays a role in the project or if there are virtual locations or URLs that need to be considered, it is crucial to communicate this in the prompt. By doing so, the intelligent tool can provide location-specific insights or information.

Provide the geographical or virtual location the document refers to. If a URL or location-Specific data is significant, include these in your prompts.

5.2.4 **Why**: Addressing the purpose of the document is vital to ensure that the reader comprehends the underlying rationale. By articulating the motivations, objectives, or desired outcomes, project managers enable the intelligent tool to generate outputs that align with the intended purpose.

Emphasize the purpose of the document. Understanding 'why' helps the AI tool to imbue relevance and context into its output.

5.2.5 **Who**: Identifying the stakeholders or individuals involved in the project is a crucial aspect of project management. Including information about who will be impacted by the project, who is responsible for various tasks, and who the document is intended for provides context for the intelligent tool to generate outputs that cater to the specific audience.

5.2.6 **How**: The "How" aspect in prompt engineering for project management documents focuses on the methodology, approach, or strategies to be employed in achieving project objectives. Including the "How" in the prompt provides guidance to the AI tool on the specific techniques or steps that should be considered or discussed in the output. This information helps ensure that the generated document reflects the desired methodology or approach.

Outline the step-by-step process or methodology to be followed in executing the project plan. Include key activities, milestones, dependencies, and any specific techniques or tools to be utilized.

5.2.7 **Other**: The "Other" aspect in prompt engineering allows project managers to include any additional information or specific requirements that may be unique to their project or document. It provides the flexibility to address specific considerations not covered by the other elements of the prompt. Including the "Other" aspect in the prompt allows project managers to communicate their specific expectations to the AI tool, ensuring that the generated output takes into account any additional instructions or requirements.

Other Example: Please consider including the potential risks and mitigation strategies associated with each identified benefit in the benefits register. Additionally, if there are any specific metrics or indicators to track the progress or achievement of each benefit, please include those as well.

Here is a sample prompt card using the Project Pathfinder Prompt System

PROJECT PATHFINDER PROMPT SYSTEM
Prompt
• **What - The Quest: Represents the mission or objective of the project.** • **When - The Timeline: Refers to the duration, milestones, and deadlines.** • **Where - The Terrain: Indicates the location or environment of the project, whether it's physical or virtual.** • **Why - The Motive: Stands for the purpose or rationale of the project.** • **Who - The Crew: Highlights the team members or stakeholders involved.** • **How - The Blueprint: Describes the approach or methodology to achieve the objectives.** • **Format - The Framework: Specifies the structural design or layout of the project.** • **Other pertinent information - The Compass Notes: Includes any additional details or contextual information important for project navigation.**

Table 1: Simple Project Pathfinder Prompt Example

5.3: Designing the Document's Structure

Lastly, the configuration of the document, be it in rows, columns, lines, or any other format, is a detail not to be overlooked. An AI tool can produce the document in a layout you prefer if it's correctly instructed. Visual design can play an important role in information comprehension, so your prompts should include guidance for the AI on the desired layout. If there is a particular way in which the project management document should be organized, it is crucial to provide instructions to the intelligent tool. Whether it involves rows and columns, specific line breaks, or other configurations, clear guidelines will aid in producing an output that closely resembles the project manager's vision.

Developing effective prompts for project management documents and plans requires careful consideration of every aspect and detail. By incorporating the 5W's, including the "Who" aspect, and providing clear instructions on formatting and configuration, project managers can optimize the use of intelligent tools like ChatGPT and Google Bard.

Through detailed prompts, you can harness the impressive capabilities of AI tools in your project management endeavors. By treating the AI tool as a valuable team member that needs clear instructions, you'll find that the quality of the output is directly proportional to the clarity and detail of the input. Remember, the more specific you are with your AI tool, the better it will serve you.

Throughout this book, we will explore the practicalities of querying AI tools for optimized results, where we'll continue to review the relationship between user instructions and AI output.

CHAPTER SIX: PREDICTIVE PROJECT MANAGEMENT PROMPTS

> *"A great prompt engineer is like an alchemist, transforming uncertainty into actionable insights, and turning project challenges into golden opportunities."*

Having gained a solid understanding of prompt engineering and how to effectively prompt AI tools, it is now time to get into practical exercises that demonstrate the application of these techniques in project management.

In this section, we will explore how to prompt AI tools to generate various project management documents such as project charters, benefits registers, plans, reports, and more.

By providing prompt cards and comparing the outputs, project managers can refine their skills in extracting the most valuable data from AI tools. Let's begin with our first example: the project charter.

6.1 Prompting the AI Tool for a Project Charter:

6.1.1 Understanding the Project Charter: The project charter is a familiar document in project management that outlines the project's purpose, objectives, scope, stakeholders, and initial requirements. It serves as a foundation for project initiation and ensures alignment between project teams and key stakeholders.

6.1.2 Crafting the Prompt Card: To prompt the AI tool effectively, project managers can use a prompt card that includes specific fields and information relevant to the project charter. The prompt card provides a structured guide for extracting the desired data from the AI tool. Here's an example of a simple prompt card for a project charter:

PROJECT CHARTER PROMPT
Create a project charter for a Microsoft Office 365 refresh project with the following fields:<ul><li>Project Overview</li><li>Project Scope</li><li>Project Objectives</li><li>Stakeholders</li><li>Project Timeline</li><li>Budget</li><li>Project Risks and Mitigation</li><li>Sign-off (stakeholders: sponsor, project manager, steering committee)</li><li>Format: Table with rows and columns</li></ul>

Table 2: Simple Project Charter Prompt Example

You could take this prompt as is by copying the entire thing and pasting it into the AI tool. for example this is what it would look like in ChatGPT.

Figure 1: Example of Project Charter Prompt in ChatGPT

Results & Discussion

- What output did the system generate for you?

- Try tweaking your prompt card to include some dummy data. Did the output vary?

6.2 Prompt Engineering Maturity

When you become proficient in prompt engineering, it means you've developed an understanding of how to frame questions or statements to elicit the most relevant and useful responses from AI models, such as Project Pathfinder System.

However, while the Project Pathfinder System provides a structured guideline to help you create prompts with the necessary aspects like 'The Quest', 'The Timeline', 'The Terrain', 'The Motive', 'The Crew', 'The Blueprint', 'The Framework', and 'The Compass Notes', you don't need to follow it verbatim as you mature in prompt engineering. This is because every project is unique, and the exact information you need might vary from project to project. For instance, in some cases, 'The Terrain' might not be as relevant, or 'The Crew' might need more emphasis. Similarly, the way you phrase your prompts can be more dynamic and adaptable, based on the context of your project.

Therefore, even if you're not using the exact wording from the Project Pathfinder System, you can still utilize its principles to create effective prompts. For instance, you can frame your prompts to focus on understanding the project's objectives, deadlines, environment, purpose, team, approach, layout, and any other pertinent details.

In other words, the Project Pathfinder System is more about understanding the essential elements of information necessary for successful project management, rather than following a strict script. Once you've mastered these principles, you can use your creativity and judgment to design prompts that are specifically tailored to your unique project management needs.

Here is an example of a project charter prompt card that aligns with the Pathfinder Prompt System while capturing the essence of the system variables:

PROJECT CHARTER PROMPT CARD (PATHFINDER PROMPT SYSTEM)
1. Purpose: Clearly state the primary purpose and objectives of the project, addressing the "What" aspect.
2. Scope: Define the boundaries and deliverables of the project, specifying what is included and excluded.
3. Stakeholders: Identify the key stakeholders involved in the project, including both internal and external parties.
4. Requirements: Describe the initial requirements and constraints of the project, considering both functional and non-functional aspects.
5. Timeline: Provide an estimated timeline for project completion, highlighting key milestones and dependencies, incorporating the "When" aspect.
6. Risks: Identify potential risks or challenges associated with the project, assessing their impact and probability.
7. Success Criteria: Define the criteria that will determine the success of the project, including specific metrics or indicators to measure achievement.
8. Communication Plan: Outline the approach for effective communication and collaboration among project stakeholders, considering both formal and informal channels.
9. Resources: Identify the key resources required to execute the project, including personnel, equipment, facilities, and budget considerations.
10. Signatories: List the authorized individuals who approve and sign off on the project charter, ensuring appropriate governance and accountability.

By aligning with the Pathfinder Prompt System, this prompt card covers all the essential aspects of a project charter, ensuring that the necessary information is provided for generating a comprehensive project charter document.

By aligning with the Pathfinder Prompt System, this prompt card covers all the essential aspects of a project charter, ensuring that the necessary information is provided for generating a comprehensive project charter document. Here is a completed version of the prompt card now ready to be entered into ChatGPT or your AI system.

For best results, start off with the over-arching command:

//GENERATE A DETAILED PROJECT CHARTER WITH THESE PARAMETERS. USE DUMMY DATA AS NEEDED//

PROJECT CHARTER PROMPT CARD (PATHFINDER PROMPT SYSTEM)

1. Purpose: This project entails a Microsoft Office 365 software refresh for the City of Phoenix, Arizona.
2. Scope: The scope of this project is limited to the IT department workers in the Motor Vehicle Division.
3. Stakeholders: The key stakeholders for this project include the Chief Information Officer (CIO) and other local workers.
4. Requirements: The project requires the procurement and deployment of 5000 machines for the software refresh.
5. Timeline: The project timeline spans from June 2023 to February 2024, allowing for a comprehensive implementation.
6. Success Criteria: The success criteria for this project are defined as the successful implementation of the software refresh, ensuring that all systems are up and running without any major issues.
7. Communication Plan: The communication plan for this project involves weekly reports for the stakeholders and daily stand-up meetings for the project team. Additional ad hoc meetings will be scheduled as necessary.
8. Resources: The key resources for this project will be provided by the vendors' IT department. The City of Phoenix will contribute minimum inputs required for the project.
9. Signatories: The signatories for the project charter include the CIO, the Mayor's office, other relevant stakeholders, and power users.
10. Other: TABULAR FORMAT SHOULD BE GENERATED FOR THIS DOCUMENT

You could take this prompt as is by copying the entire thing and pasting it into the AI tool. for example this is what it would look like in ChatGPT.

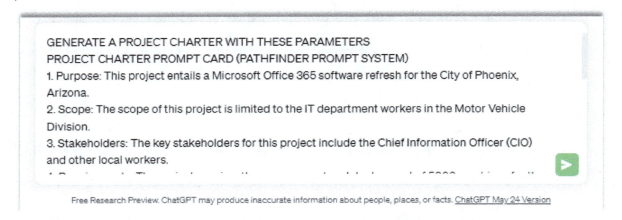

GENERATE A PROJECT CHARTER WITH THESE PARAMETERS
PROJECT CHARTER PROMPT CARD (PATHFINDER PROMPT SYSTEM)
1. Purpose: This project entails a Microsoft Office 365 software refresh for the City of Phoenix, Arizona.
2. Scope: The scope of this project is limited to the IT department workers in the Motor Vehicle Division.
3. Stakeholders: The key stakeholders for this project include the Chief Information Officer (CIO) and other local workers.

Free Research Preview. ChatGPT may produce inaccurate information about people, places, or facts. ChatGPT May 24 Version

Figure 2: Example of Project Charter Prompt in ChatGPT

If at any point, the prompt fails to yield the desired output - say, in a table format, there are a couple of options available to you. You could either halt the generation process midway or allow the initial iteration of data to be produced before intervening with a new prompt.

A suitable command to reprompt could be something along the lines of // The entire prompt needs to be presented in a tabular format. Kindly redo //. When you issue this command, ChatGPT will make a new attempt to reformat and regenerate your content, and it might even extend an apology for not getting it right the first time. Let's explore the type of output this reiteration process can help you obtain.

6.3 Using the Prompt Card with the AI Tool

Copy the prompt card and paste it into an AI tool like ChatGPT or any other reliable and tested AI tool. Then, compare the generated output with the expected data from the prompt card. This exercise helps project managers refine their prompt engineering skills by analyzing the AI-generated content.

Output

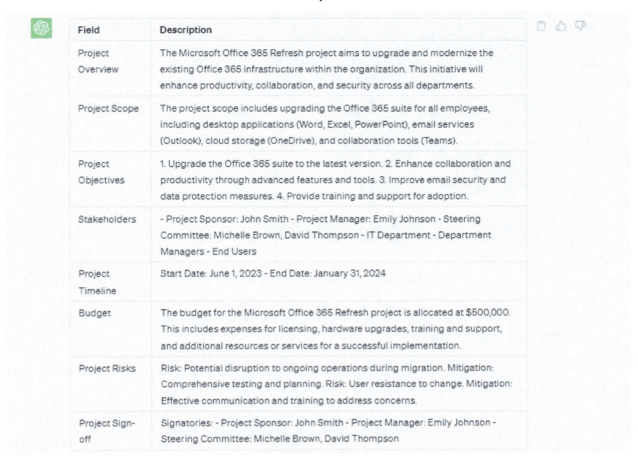

Field	Description
Project Overview	The Microsoft Office 365 Refresh project aims to upgrade and modernize the existing Office 365 infrastructure within the organization. This initiative will enhance productivity, collaboration, and security across all departments.
Project Scope	The project scope includes upgrading the Office 365 suite for all employees, including desktop applications (Word, Excel, PowerPoint), email services (Outlook), cloud storage (OneDrive), and collaboration tools (Teams).
Project Objectives	1. Upgrade the Office 365 suite to the latest version. 2. Enhance collaboration and productivity through advanced features and tools. 3. Improve email security and data protection measures. 4. Provide training and support for adoption.
Stakeholders	- Project Sponsor: John Smith - Project Manager: Emily Johnson - Steering Committee: Michelle Brown, David Thompson - IT Department - Department Managers - End Users
Project Timeline	Start Date: June 1, 2023 - End Date: January 31, 2024
Budget	The budget for the Microsoft Office 365 Refresh project is allocated at $500,000. This includes expenses for licensing, hardware upgrades, training and support, and additional resources or services for a successful implementation.
Project Risks	Risk: Potential disruption to ongoing operations during migration. Mitigation: Comprehensive testing and planning. Risk: User resistance to change. Mitigation: Effective communication and training to address concerns.
Project Sign-off	Signatories: - Project Sponsor: John Smith - Project Manager: Emily Johnson - Steering Committee: Michelle Brown, David Thompson

Figure 3: Generated Output Example

6.4 How To Copy A Table From Chatgpt When The Copy-Button Output Is Undesirable

For optimal visualization of the generated data, it is recommended that you manually copy the table. This can be achieved by selecting the entire table before pressing the copy button. Relying on the shortcut copy button, located at the top-right of the output display, may not produce a satisfactory or desired result.

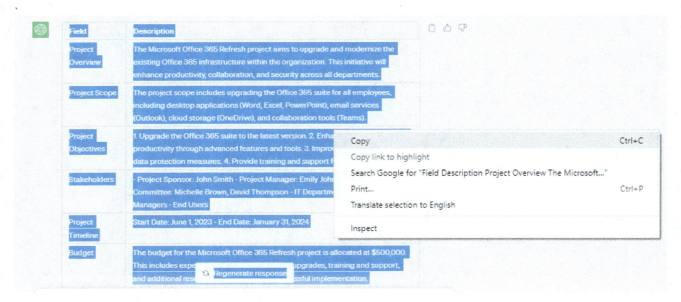

Figure 4: How to copy a table from ChatGPT

6.5 Project Charter Exercise Output

The final output from ChatGPT for the sample project charter is presented here, demonstrating its capability to synthesize data based on the input given. However, the quality and depth of the output can greatly depend on the complexity of the prompt card.

Paradoxically, it has been found that a succinct, less detailed prompt card can **occasionally** yield a more comprehensive output than an intricate one. This arises from the dynamic and context-dependent nature of the underlying model, implying that one cannot anticipate identical results every time. It requires a flexible approach, with a readiness to adapt, re-ask, or even completely overhaul the system's prompts to obtain optimal results.

Field	Description
Project Overview	The Microsoft Office 365 Refresh project aims to upgrade and modernize the existing Office 365 infrastructure within the organization. This initiative will enhance productivity, collaboration, and security across all departments.
Project Scope	The project scope includes upgrading the Office 365 suite for all employees, including desktop applications (Word, Excel, PowerPoint), email services (Outlook), cloud storage (OneDrive), and collaboration tools (Teams).
Project Objectives	1. Upgrade the Office 365 suite to the latest version. 2. Enhance collaboration and productivity through advanced features and tools. 3. Improve email security and data protection measures. 4. Provide training and support for adoption.
Stakeholders	- Project Sponsor: John Smith - Project Manager: Emily Johnson - Steering Committee: Michelle Brown, David Thompson - IT Department - Department Managers - End Users
Project Timeline	Start Date: June 1, 2023 - End Date: January 31, 2024
Budget	The budget for the Microsoft Office 365 Refresh project is allocated at $500,000. This includes expenses for licensing, hardware upgrades, training and support, and additional resources or services for a successful implementation.
Project Risks	Risk: Potential disruption to ongoing operations during migration. Mitigation: Comprehensive testing and planning. Risk: User resistance to change. Mitigation: Effective communication and training to address concerns.
Project Sign-off	Signatories: - Project Sponsor: John Smith - Project Manager: Emily Johnson - Steering Committee: Michelle Brown, David Thompson

For instance, in the first experiment, a comprehensive prompt card produced a terse project charter that lacked in-depth detail. In contrast, when the system was prompted to deliver a **"DETAILED"** project charter using **"MOCK DATA"**, ChatGPT was observed to be more adept at contributing innovative ideas, unhindered by the constraints of an overly detailed prompt card.

Here is the modified prompt entered into ChatGPT

 GENERATE A DETAILED PROJECT CHARTER WITH THESE PARAMETERS. USE DUMMY DATA AS NEEDED

PROJECT CHARTER PROMPT CARD (PATHFINDER PROMPT SYSTEM)

1. Purpose: This project entails a Microsoft Office 365 software refresh for the City of Phoenix, Arizona.

2. Scope: The scope of this project is limited to the IT department workers in the Motor Vehicle Division.

3. Stakeholders: The key stakeholders for this project include the Chief Information Officer (CIO) and other local workers.

4. Requirements: The project requires the procurement and deployment of 5000 machines for the software refresh.

5. Timeline: The project timeline spans from June 2023 to February 2024, allowing for a comprehensive implementation.

6. Success Criteria: The success criteria for this project are defined as the successful implementation of the software refresh, ensuring that all systems are up and running without any major issues.

7. Communication Plan: The communication plan for this project involves weekly reports for the stakeholders and daily stand-up meetings for the project team. Additional ad hoc meetings will be scheduled as necessary.

8. Resources: The key resources for this project will be provided by the vendors' IT department. The City of Phoenix will contribute minimum inputs required for the project.

9. Signatories: The signatories for the project charter include the CIO, the Mayor's office, other relevant stakeholders, and power users.

10. Other: TABULAR FORMAT SHOULD BE GENERATED FOR THIS DOCUMENT

↻ Regenerate response

Send a message ➤

Here is the raw output from ChatGPT

PROJECT CHARTER

Project Title: Microsoft Office 365 Software Refresh Project

Location: City of Phoenix, Arizona

Project Start Date: June 1, 2023

Project End Date: February 28, 2024

I. Purpose

The purpose of this project is to execute a comprehensive Microsoft Office 365 software refresh for the IT department workers in the Motor Vehicle Division of the City of Phoenix, Arizona.

II. Scope

This project involves the IT department workers in the Motor Vehicle Division. It includes the procurement and deployment of 5000 new machines for the software refresh.

III. Stakeholders

The primary stakeholders for this project include:

1. The Chief Information Officer (CIO)
2. The IT department staff
3. Other local workers in the Motor Vehicle Division

IV. Requirements

The requirements for this project include:

1. Procurement of 5000 new machines for the software refresh
2. Setup and deployment of the new software on these machines
3. Training the staff to use the updated software

V. Timeline

The project spans from June 2023 to February 2024, providing a nine-month window for a thorough implementation of the software refresh.

VI. Success Criteria

The project will be deemed successful upon:

1. Successful procurement and deployment of the 5000 machines
2. Successful software refresh on all machines
3. Absence of any major operational issues post-refresh
4. Positive feedback from staff on the performance and usability of the updated software

VII. Communication Plan

The communication plan involves:

1. Weekly progress reports to stakeholders
2. Daily stand-up meetings for the project team
3. Ad hoc meetings scheduled as necessary

VIII. Resources

The key resources for this project will be provided by the vendors' IT department. The City of Phoenix will contribute the minimum inputs required for the project.

IX. Signatories

The project charter signatories include:

1. The Chief Information Officer (CIO)
2. Representatives from the Mayor's Office
3. Key stakeholders
4. Power users

Please note that by signing, each party acknowledges their understanding of the charter and commits to its terms.

Signatory	Name	Date
CIO	TBD	TBD
Mayor's Office Representative	TBD	TBD
Stakeholder	TBD	TBD
Power User	TBD	TBD

X. Other

Additional sections or modifications to this charter may be made as deemed necessary by the project team and stakeholders.

 The vast difference in output demonstrates the importance of understanding the model's behavior in different contexts, and using this knowledge to guide interactions for optimal outcomes.

Format your project charter using spreadsheet software and compare with results on the pages ahead.

PROJECT CHARTER	
Project Title: Microsoft Office 365 Software Refresh Project	
Location: City of Phoenix, Arizona	
Project Start Date: June 1, 2023	
Project End Date: February 28, 2024	
I. Purpose	
The purpose of this project is to execute a comprehensive Microsoft Office 365 software refresh for the IT department workers in the Motor Vehicle Division of the City of Phoenix, Arizona.	
II. Scope	
This project involves the IT department workers in the Motor Vehicle Division. It includes the procurement and deployment of 5000 new machines for the software refresh.	
III. Stakeholders	
The primary stakeholders for this project include:	
1. The Chief Information Officer (CIO)	
2. The IT department staff	
3. Other local workers in the Motor Vehicle Division	
IV. Requirements	
The requirements for this project include:	
1. Procurement of 5000 new machines for the software refresh	
2. Setup and deployment of the new software on these machines	
3. Training the staff to use the updated software	
V. Timeline	
The project spans from June 2023 to February 2024, providing a nine-month window for a thorough implementation of the software refresh.	
VI. Success Criteria	
The project will be deemed successful upon:	
1. Successful procurement and deployment of the 5000 machines	
2. Successful software refresh on all machines	
3. Absence of any major operational issues post-refresh	
4. Positive feedback from staff on the performance and usability of the updated software	
VII. Communication Plan	
The communication plan involves:	
1. Weekly progress reports to stakeholders	
2. Daily stand-up meetings for the project team	
3. Ad hoc meetings scheduled as necessary	
VIII. Resources	
The key resources for this project will be provided by the vendors' IT department. The City of Phoenix will contribute the minimum inputs required for the project.	
IX. Signatories	
The project charter signatories include:	
1. The Chief Information Officer (CIO)	
2. Representatives from the Mayor's Office	
3. Key stakeholders	
4. Power users	
Please note that by signing, each party acknowledges their understanding of the charter and commits to its terms.	

Signatory	Name
CIO	TBD
Mayor's Office Representative	TBD
Stakeholder	TBD
Power User	TBD

Table 3: Sample Formatted Project Charter from ChatGPT

Project Charter Example
Project Title: Implementation of a Customer Relationship Management System
Project Overview
The purpose of this project is to implement a Customer Relationship Management (CRM) system to improve our organization's customer service and increase customer satisfaction. The project aims to centralize customer information, streamline communication, and enhance our ability to track customer interactions.
Project Scope
Project Scope: The project will include the installation, configuration, and customization of the CRM system. The scope also covers the training of staff on the new system, data migration from the current system to the new system, and ongoing maintenance and support.
Project Objectives
• Implement a CRM system within the next six months • Centralize customer data to improve efficiency and accuracy • Enhance customer service by streamlining communication and tracking customer interactions • Increase customer satisfaction by providing better and more personalized service
Stakeholders
• Project Sponsor: CEO • Project Manager: Marketing Director • Project Team: IT Manager, Customer Service Manager, Sales Manager, Marketing Manager • External stakeholders: Customers, vendors, and partners

Project Timeline	
Week 1-2	Project planning and kick-off meeting
Week 3-4	CRM system research and selection
Week 5-8	System installation, configuration, and customization
Week 9-10	Data migration from the current system to the new system
Week 11-12	User training and system testing
Week 13-26	Ongoing maintenance and support

Budget
Budget: The total budget for this project is $150,000, which includes the cost of the CRM system, installation and customization, training, data migration, and ongoing maintenance and support.
Project Risks and Mitigation
- Technical challenges in system implementation and data migration: This risk will be mitigated by involving experienced IT professionals, testing the system before implementation, and having a backup plan in case of any failures. - Resistance to change from employees: This risk will be mitigated by involving employees in the decision-making process, providing comprehensive training and support, and addressing any concerns promptly.
Sign-off

Project Sponsor: [signature]	
Project Manager: [signature]	
Project Team: [signature]	
External stakeholders: [signature]	

Table 4: Formatted CRM Project Charter from ChatGPT

6.6 The Project Management Advantage

Once you've constructed a thorough project charter, it serves as a robust blueprint of your project, which can be utilized as a primary input for creating all other necessary project documents. This concept is what I term as the 'project management advantage'.

The advantage lies in the ability of ChatGPT, given its extensive data training and being a large language model, to comprehend the project you're working on thoroughly. ChatGPT can expand upon your project charter across various dimensions that might be challenging to do without a team of additional members.

Let's illustrate this idea: your project charter can be employed as a comprehensive prompt for generating further project documentation. Since the detailed project charter already accomplishes the 'heavy lifting', your role now shifts to maintaining consistency in your interaction with ChatGPT.

To harness the full potential of this tool, you need to remain on the same ChatGPT page instance that your project charter was developed on. The reason behind this is that the prior conversations you've had with ChatGPT while crafting this project charter have primed it to comprehend your project's nuances. This understanding allows it to produce an array of project documents based on simple additional prompts.

To further illustrate this, we will explore additional documentation that ChatGPT can generate for us, using the same instance in which the project charter was developed. The crucial point here is consistency in using the same ChatGPT instance for the best results, a conclusion derived from my personal experience with this tool.

At this stage, you might not need to fully utilize the pathway model unless the AI tool encounters a challenge or fails to comprehend the context of the documentation you're attempting to produce. This lack of understanding is usually evident when it struggles to generate coherent output.

In these scenarios, turn to your Project Management Body of Knowledge (PMBOK® Guide). List out the specific variables or components integral to the document you're trying to create, which will assist in guiding ChatGPT's response. By doing so, you'll enhance its contextual understanding and facilitate more accurate and relevant outputs.

6.7 Develop a Scope Management Plan: Using the following prompt, create a Scope Management Plan. Just copy the text in between the "//" tags. There is no need to add anything else.

SCOPE MANAGEMENT PLAN PROMPT
//Based on the information I have shared with you about this project, create for me a project scope management plan using dummy data. Display in a tabular format.//

SCOPE MANAGEMENT PLAN	
Section	**Details**
Project Title	Microsoft Office 365 Software Refresh Project
Scope Management Plan Purpose	To define the processes that will be used to identify, define, validate, and control the project scope
Scope Definition	A software refresh of Microsoft Office 365 for IT department workers in the Motor Vehicle Division, including the procurement and deployment of 5000 new machines
Roles & Responsibilities	1. **Project Manager**: Ensure the project scope is defined, approved, and managed. 2. **CIO**: Provide guidance, approve the project scope, and monitor project progress. 3. **IT Department Staff**: Support the execution of project tasks and provide technical expertise
Scope Identification Process	1. **Requirement Gathering**: Understand the requirements of all stakeholders 2. **Scope Definition**: Define the scope based on the requirements gathered
Scope Validation Process	1. **Preliminary Scope Statement Review**: Review by key stakeholders 2. **Final Scope Statement Approval**: Approval by project sponsor (CIO)
Scope Control Process	1. **Scope Baseline Establishment**: Create a baseline scope statement 2. **Scope Change Management**: Handle requests for changes to the project scope
Change Request Process	All change requests should be submitted to the Project Manager, who will review them with the project team and CIO for approval or denial
Acceptance Criteria	The project is considered successful when all machines have been procured and deployed, the software refresh is complete, there are no major operational issues, and feedback from staff is positive

Table 5: Scope Management Plan from ChatGPT

6.8 Develop a Requirements Management Plan: Using the following prompt

REQUIREMENTS MANAGEMENT PLAN PROMPT

//Based on the information I have shared with you about this project, create for me a Requirements Management Plan using dummy data. Add typical requirements-oriented concerns.//

REQUIREMENTS MANAGEMENT PLAN	
Section	**Details**
Project Title	Microsoft Office 365 Software Refresh Project
Plan Purpose	The purpose of this plan is to establish a common understanding of how the requirements for the Microsoft Office 365 Software Refresh Project will be identified, analyzed, documented, and managed.
Requirements Identification	Requirements will be identified through stakeholder interviews, technical assessments, and existing documentation. Stakeholders include the CIO, IT department staff, and selected power users.
Requirement Analysis	The identified requirements will be analyzed to determine their relevance, feasibility, and level of priority. This will be done by the project manager, with inputs from the CIO and IT department staff.
Requirements Documentation	All the identified and analyzed requirements will be documented in a Requirements Traceability Matrix (RTM). The RTM will include information such as the source of the requirement, priority, status, and any relevant comments.
Requirements Management Tools	We will utilize a combination of collaboration tools for effective requirements management. These include Microsoft Excel for the RTM, and a project management platform for tracking and communication.
Requirements Traceability	To ensure traceability, every requirement will be uniquely identified in the RTM. Changes to the requirements will be logged, and the impacts analyzed before approval.
Requirements Communication	The RTM will be shared with all stakeholders. Any changes to requirements will be communicated to all relevant parties, typically through email notifications and during project meetings.
Change Control Process	Any changes to the established requirements will go through a formal change control process which includes documenting the proposed change, analyzing its impact, reviewing it with stakeholders, and obtaining necessary approvals.
Requirements Validation	Requirements will be validated by the stakeholders through regular reviews of the RTM. At project completion, the delivered solution will be validated against the documented requirements to ensure all have been met.
Roles and Responsibilities	**Project Manager**: Oversee requirements management process **CIO**: Provide strategic direction and approve changes **IT Department Staff**: Identify, analyze, and validate requirements **Power Users**: Assist in validating requirements
Typical Requirement-Oriented Concerns	1. Changes in business needs leading to scope changes 2. Incomplete or ambiguous requirements 3. Miscommunication or misunderstanding of requirements 4. Stakeholder disagreement on requirements

Table 6: Requirements Management Plan from ChatGPT

6.9 Develop a Requirements Traceability Matrix: Using the following prompt

<table>
<tr><td style="background-color:#7aa858">REQUIREMENTS TRACEABILITY MATRIX PROMPT</td></tr>
<tr><td>//Based on the information I have shared with you about this project, create for me a requirements traceability matrix using dummy data. Add use-case, test-script, requestor and other requirements-relevant variables.//</td></tr>
</table>

REQUIREMENTS TRACEABILITY MATRIX						
Requirement ID	Requirement Description	Use-Case	Test Script ID	Requestor	Priority	Status
REQ-001	Procure 5000 new machines	Use-Case-001	TS-001	CIO	High	In progress
REQ-002	Install and set up Microsoft Office 365 on all new machines	Use-Case-002	TS-002	IT Manager	High	Not started
REQ-003	Conduct training sessions for IT department staff	Use-Case-003	TS-003	IT Staff Member	Medium	Not started
REQ-004	Prepare a comprehensive final report on the implementation process	Use-Case-004	TS-004	Project Manager	Medium	Not started
REQ-005	Ensure minimal operational issues post-refresh	Use-Case-005	TS-005	CIO	High	Not started
REQ-006	Achieve positive feedback from staff post-implementation	Use-Case-006	TS-006	Power User	Low	Not star

Table 7: Requirements Traceability Matrix from ChatGPT

6. 10 Develop a Project Scope Statement: Using the following prompt

PROJECT SCOPE STATEMENT PROMPT

//Based on the information I have shared with you about this project, create for me a project scope statement using dummy data. Also add inclusions, exclusions and detailed deliverable descriptions in addition to acceptance criteria. In a table format.//

PROJECT SCOPE STATEMENT	
Section	**Details**
Project Title	Microsoft Office 365 Software Refresh Project
Project Description	This project aims to conduct a comprehensive software refresh of Microsoft Office 365 for the IT department workers in the Motor Vehicle Division of the City of Phoenix, Arizona. This encompasses the procurement and deployment of 5000 new machines.
Project Inclusions	1. Procurement of 5000 new machines 2. Installation and setup of Microsoft Office 365 on all new machines 3. Training sessions for IT department staff on the updated software 4. A comprehensive final report on the implementation process
Project Exclusions	1. Physical setup of new machines 2. Support for non-Microsoft Office 365 software 3. Training for departments outside the IT department
Detailed Deliverables	1. **5000 new machines**: These machines will replace old ones and will be equipped with the latest version of Microsoft Office 365. 2. **Installation and Setup**: The new machines will be set up with Microsoft Office 365 software. 3. **Training Sessions**: The IT department staff will be trained on how to use and troubleshoot the updated software. 4. **Final Report**: A comprehensive report detailing the implementation process, challenges encountered, and their solutions will be prepared.
Project Acceptance Criteria	1. Successful procurement and setup of all 5000 new machines 2. Successful completion of the Microsoft Office 365 software refresh on all machines 3. Minimal operational issues post-refresh 4. Positive feedback received from staff post-implementation

Table 8: Project Scope Statement from ChatGPT

6. 11 Develop a Work Breakdown Structure: Using the following prompt

<table>
<tr><td>WBS PROMPT PROMPT</td></tr>
<tr><td>//Based on the information I have shared with you about this project, create for me a WBS using dummy data. Create a detailed WBS of at least 3 levels. Make it visual and hierarchical.//</td></tr>
</table>

Output

Microsoft Office 365 Software Refresh Project

1. Project Management
    1. Project Planning
        - Scope Management
        - Time Management
        - Cost Management
        - Quality Management
        - Communication Management
        - Risk Management
        - Procurement Management
    2. Project Monitoring and Control
        - Progress Reporting
        - Change Management
        - Risk Monitoring and Control
        - Quality Control
        - Issue Resolution
    3. Project Closing
        - Project Review
        - Documentation Archiving
        - Post-Project Review
2. Procurement of Machines
    1. Vendor Selection
        - Market Research
        - Vendor Evaluation and Selection
    2. Machine Procurement
        - Create Purchase Orders

- Receive and Inspect Machines

3. Software Refresh

    1. Installation and Setup

- Software Installation
- System Testing

    2. User Training

- Develop Training Materials
- Conduct Training Sessions

    3. Post-Implementation Support

- Troubleshooting Support
- Feedback Collection

Entering this data into PowerPoint, we can obtain the results shown on the following page.

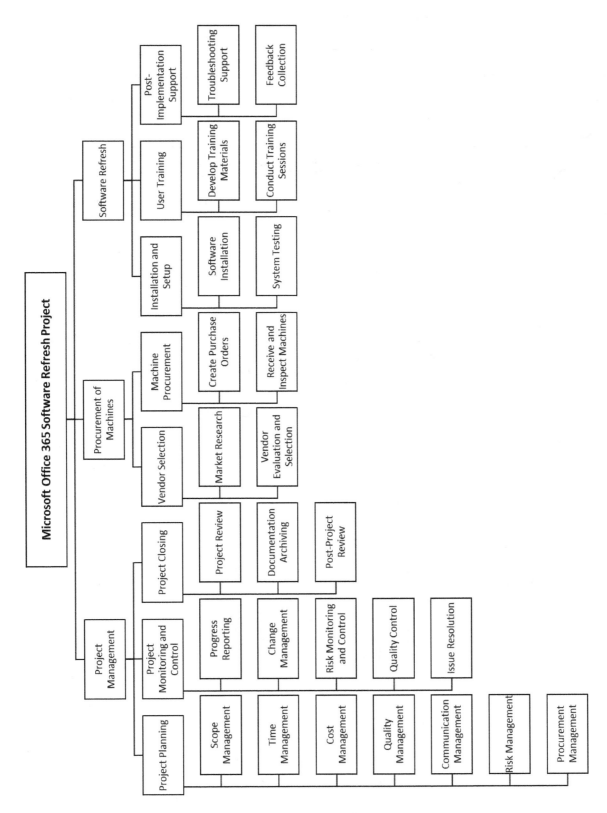

Table 9: WBS from ChatGPT-Generated Data & Powerpoint

6. 12 Develop a Deliverable Acceptance Form: Using the following prompt

<table>
<tr><td style="background:#8cc63f">DELIVERABLE ACCEPTANCE FORM PROMPT</td></tr>
<tr><td>//Based on the information I have shared with you about this project, create for me a DETAILED Deliverable Acceptance Form using dummy data.//</td></tr>
</table>

<table>
<tr><td colspan="7" align="center">DELIVERABLE ACCEPTANCE FORM</td></tr>
<tr>
<th>Deliverable ID</th>
<th>Deliverable Description</th>
<th>Criteria</th>
<th>Status</th>
<th>Date Delivered</th>
<th>Accepted (Yes/No)</th>
<th>Signature</th>
</tr>
<tr>
<td>DEL-001</td>
<td>Procurement of 5000 new machines</td>
<td>Machines meet technical specs, quantity is correct, all machines are functioning</td>
<td>Complete</td>
<td>15-Aug-23</td>
<td>Yes</td>
<td>[Signature]</td>
</tr>
<tr>
<td>DEL-002</td>
<td>Installation and setup of Microsoft Office 365 on all machines</td>
<td>All machines have Office 365 installed, licenses activated, all apps functioning as expected</td>
<td>In Progress</td>
<td>22-Aug-23</td>
<td>Pending</td>
<td></td>
</tr>
<tr>
<td>DEL-003</td>
<td>Conducting training sessions for IT department staff</td>
<td>All IT department staff trained, all users comfortable with the software, pre- and post-training evaluation scores meet the acceptable threshold</td>
<td>Not started</td>
<td>TBD</td>
<td>No</td>
<td></td>
</tr>
<tr>
<td>DEL-004</td>
<td>Comprehensive final report on the implementation process</td>
<td>Final report complete, includes all implementation details, challenges, resolutions, lessons learned, and recommendations</td>
<td>Not started</td>
<td>TBD</td>
<td>No</td>
<td></td>
</tr>
<tr>
<td>DEL-005</td>
<td>Minimal operational issues post-refresh</td>
<td>Number of issues reported is below acceptable threshold, all major issues resolved within the agreed time-frame</td>
<td>Not started</td>
<td>TBD</td>
<td>No</td>
<td></td>
</tr>
<tr>
<td>DEL-006</td>
<td>Positive feedback from staff post-implementation</td>
<td>Feedback survey results meet the acceptable threshold for user satisfaction</td>
<td>Not started</td>
<td>TBD</td>
<td>No</td>
<td></td>
</tr>
</table>

Table 10: Deliverable Acceptance Form from ChatGPT

We've so far explored the strategic use of prompts to facilitate effective scope management in the realm of predictive project management. We've seen how carefully crafted prompts can help generate crucial artifacts related to this knowledge area. The same methodology can be applied to all knowledge areas within project management.

By maintaining a consistent interaction within the same session with ChatGPT, you can instruct the AI to generate relevant artifacts for each and every knowledge area. In the following sections of this guide, we will explore examples of this methodology applied to various knowledge areas, illustrating how you can leverage the capabilities of ChatGPT to streamline and enhance your project management processes.

6. 13 Create an Assumption Log: Using the following prompt

ASSUMPTION LOG PROMPT

//Based on the information I have shared with you about this project, create for me a DETAILED Assumption Log using dummy data.//

ASSUMPTION LOG							
Assumption ID	**Assumption**	**Reason for Assumption**	**Impact (If False)**	**Owner**	**Date Identified**	**Date Validated**	**Status**
A-001	All 5000 machines will be ready for deployment within two months.	Vendor's previous track record.	Project delay, may impact other departments' schedules.	[Owner's Name]	15-Jun-23	TBD	Open
A-002	The vendor can provide the necessary technical support during the deployment.	Vendor has confirmed in initial discussions.	Additional internal resources might be required, which could increase the project cost.	[Owner's Name]	18-Jun-23	TBD	Open
A-003	The existing IT infrastructure is sufficient to support the new software.	Based on recent IT audit results.	Additional upgrades might be necessary, potentially increasing the cost and timeline of the project.	[Owner's Name]	20-Jun-23	TBD	Open
A-004	All IT department staff can be trained on the new software within a month.	Based on the complexity of the software and the staff's previous learning curve.	May require additional training sessions, which could delay full implementation.	[Owner's Name]	25-Jun-23	TBD	Open

Table 11:Assumption Log from ChatGPT

6. 14 Schedule Management Prompts

Create a: Using the following prompt

PROJECT SCHEDULE PROMPT

//Based on the information I have shared with you about this project, create for me a DETAILED Project Schedule using dummy data.//

PROJECT SCHEDULE							
Activity ID	Activity Name	Description	Predecessor	Start Date	End Date	Duration	Responsible
A1	Project Initiation	Kick-off meeting, project charter approval	N/A	1-Jun-23	5-Jun-23	5 days	Project Manager
A2	Procurement Planning	Identifying vendors, sending out RFPs	A1	6-Jun-23	10-Jun-23	5 days	Procurement Manager
A3	Vendor Selection	Reviewing proposals, selecting vendor	A2	11-Jun-23	15-Jun-23	5 days	Procurement Manager, Project Manager
A4	Procurement of Machines	Ordering, delivery, and setup of machines	A3	16-Jun-23	31-Aug-23	77 days	Vendor, IT Department
A5	Software Installation	Installation of Office 365 software on new machines	A4	1-Sep-23	15-Sep-23	15 days	Vendor, IT Department
A6	Staff Training	Training sessions for IT department staff	A5	16-Sep-23	30-Sep-23	15 days	Training Lead, IT Department
A7	Testing and Quality Assurance	Testing of software on new machines, troubleshooting	A6	1-Oct-23	15-Oct-23	15 days	QA Team, IT Department
A8	Project Closure	Final report, lessons learned, project closure	A7	16-Oct-23	31-Oct-23	16 days	Project Manager

Table 12: Project Schedule From ChatGPT

6. 15 Cost Management Prompts

Create a Project Budget Sheet: Using the following prompt

PROJECT BUDGET PROMPT

//Based on the information I have shared with you about this project, create for me a DETAILED project itemized budget for the same schedule using dummy data.//

PROJECT BUDGET			
Activity ID	**Activity Name**	**Description**	**Estimated Cost**
A1	Project Initiation	Kick-off meeting, project charter approval	$5,000
A2	Procurement Planning	Identifying vendors, sending out RFPs	$3,000
A3	Vendor Selection	Reviewing proposals, selecting vendor	$2,000
A4	Procurement of Machines	Ordering, delivery, and setup of machines (5000 machines @ $800 each)	$4,000,000
A5	Software Installation	Installation of Office 365 software on new machines (5000 machines @ $50 installation cost each)	$250,000
A6	Staff Training	Training sessions for IT department staff (25 sessions @ $500 each)	$12,500
A7	Testing and Quality Assurance	Testing of software on new machines, troubleshooting (5000 machines @ $10 testing cost each)	$50,000
A8	Project Closure	Final report, lessons learned, project closure	$3,500
Total			**$4,326,000**

Table 13: Project Budget From ChatGPT

6. 16 Create an Earned Value Sheet: Using the following prompt

EARNED VALUE ANALYSIS SHEET PROMPT

//Based on the information I have shared with you about this project, create for me a DETAILED Earned Value calculation sheet including SPI, CPI, CV, SV, PV, EV, AC and other relevant information using dummy data.//

EARNED VALUE CALCULATION SHEET							
Time Period	Planned Value (PV)	Earned Value (EV)	Actual Cost (AC)	Schedule Variance (SV = EV - PV)	Cost Variance (CV = EV - AC)	Schedule Performance Index (SPI = EV / PV)	Cost Performance Index (CPI = EV / AC)
Jun-23	$10,000	$8,000	$12,000	($2,000)	($4,000)	0.8	0.67
Jul-23	$90,000	$80,000	$100,000	($10,000)	($20,000)	0.89	0.8
Aug-23	$300,000	$320,000	$310,000	$20,000	$10,000	1.07	1.03
Sep-23	$400,000	$390,000	$410,000	($10,000)	($20,000)	0.98	0.95
Oct-23	$500,000	$480,000	$520,000	($20,000)	($40,000)	0.96	0.92

Table 14: Earned Value Calculation Sheet from ChatGPT

6. 17 Create a Quality Management Plan: Using the following prompt

QUALITY MANAGEMENT PLAN PROMPT

//Based on the information I have shared with you about this project, create for me a DETAILED Quality Management Plan using dummy data.//

QUALITY MANAGEMENT PLAN	
Section	**Description**
Quality Planning	The project will adopt the ISO 9001:2015 standard for Quality Management Systems. The aim is to ensure the successful implementation of the software refresh across all systems.
Quality Assurance	The project will establish a Quality Assurance team responsible for monitoring and ensuring adherence to the project's defined processes and standards. This team will conduct audits, perform process analysis, and ensure continuous improvement.
Quality Control	The Quality Control team will conduct checks at various stages of the project. They will verify the functionality and performance of the new software systems to ensure they meet required standards. This includes ensuring the correct installation of software and the successful transfer of data.
Quality Metrics	The project will measure the following quality metrics: 1) Percentage of systems successfully updated, 2) Number of issues identified post-implementation, 3) User satisfaction rate, 4) Downtime due to software update issues, and 5) Response time to address any issues.
Quality Improvement	This will involve identifying, analyzing, and improving upon existing weaknesses in the project. Any lessons learned will be documented and used for continuous process improvement.
Roles & Responsibilities	The Project Manager will oversee the Quality Management process. The Quality Assurance team will be responsible for upholding the quality standard throughout the project, while the Quality Control team will ensure the end product meets the specified requirements.
Tools & Techniques	The project will utilize tools such as flowcharts, checklists, and statistical process control (SPC) charts for managing quality. Pareto charts and cause-and-effect diagrams will be used to analyze and rectify any identified issues.
Documentation	All quality-related activities and results will be documented for future reference and process improvements.
Review & Audits	Quality reviews and audits will be carried out regularly to ensure that the project is following the planned quality processes and that the final product will meet the specified quality standards.
Change Management	Any changes to the quality plan will go through a change control process, which includes documenting the change, assessing the impact, approval, and communication to relevant stakeholders.

Table 15: Quality Management Plan from ChatGPT

6. 18 Create a Quality Report: Using the following prompt

QUALITY REPORT PROMPT

//Based on the information I have shared with you about this project, create for me a DETAILED Quality Report using dummy data. Include audit results, bugs and defects.//

QUALITY REPORT	
Report Section	**Description**
Quality Audit Results	Our most recent audit found that our project is adhering to the predefined quality standards and processes. There were minor non-compliance issues with documentation, which have since been addressed.
Bugs Identified	A total of 120 bugs have been identified since the project's initiation. Of these, 80 have been resolved, while 40 are in the process of being addressed. The majority of these bugs are minor and have not significantly impacted the project's progress.
Major Defects	Two major defects have been identified. The first was a compatibility issue with a specific model of desktops in use, which caused delays in the software installation. This has since been resolved by the vendor. The second defect involves a slow load time during peak usage hours, which is currently under investigation.
Quality Control Measures	Our Quality Control team is continuously monitoring the project's outputs and the software's performance. Rigorous testing protocols have been put in place to identify and rectify any bugs or defects.
Quality Assurance Findings	Our Quality Assurance team confirms that our project is aligned with the project's quality management plan. Our adherence to ISO 9001:2015 standards is satisfactory. Minor process improvements have been suggested and are currently being implemented.
Corrective Actions Taken	Corrective actions have been taken to address the minor non-compliance issues highlighted during the quality audit. These actions include staff training and process adjustments to ensure better adherence to quality standards.
Preventive Actions Taken	In response to the defects and bugs identified, preventive measures are being implemented. These include additional training for the IT department, installing updates during non-peak hours, and ensuring more rigorous testing before installation.
Recommendations for Improvement	It is recommended to increase the frequency of quality audits and to conduct more intensive pre-installation testing for complex systems. A detailed review of the software compatibility with all devices in use is also recommended.

Table 16: Quality Report from ChatGPT

6. 19 Create a Resource Management Plan: Using the following prompt

RESOURCE MANAGEMENT PLAN PROMPT

//Based on the information I have shared with you about this project, create for me a DETAILED

Resource Management Plan using dummy data.//

RESOURCE MANAGEMENT PLAN	
Section	**Description**
Roles & Responsibilities	The key roles in this project include Project Manager, IT Team, Quality Assurance Team, and Procurement Team. The Project Manager is responsible for overall project execution. The IT Team is responsible for software installation and troubleshooting. The Quality Assurance Team ensures adherence to quality standards, and the Procurement Team handles the purchasing and delivery of new machines.
Resource Identification	The project requires human resources (the teams mentioned above), as well as physical resources (5000 new machines and the necessary software licenses). The City of Phoenix IT department and vendor support are also considered resources.
Resource Estimation	Each team consists of various roles requiring different skill sets. The Project Manager will oversee 1 IT Team Lead, 10 IT Technicians, 1 Quality Assurance Lead, 2 Quality Assurance Technicians, 1 Procurement Officer, and 2 Procurement Assistants. The estimated physical resources include 5000 machines, the required software, and the facilities to accommodate the work.
Resource Acquisition	Human resources will be acquired internally within the City of Phoenix. The Procurement Team will handle the purchase of the physical resources from selected vendors.
Resource Training	Training will be provided to the IT Team on the specifics of the software refresh process. The Quality Assurance Team will be trained on the project's specific quality requirements.
Resource Scheduling	A detailed schedule will be created to ensure the optimal utilization of all resources. The Project Manager will monitor this schedule and make adjustments as needed.
Resource Monitoring & Control	The Project Manager will monitor resource usage and performance throughout the project. Regular meetings will be held to update all team members and stakeholders on resource allocation and usage.
Resource Release	At the end of the project, physical resources will be disposed of or repurposed as necessary. Human resources will be released back to their departments or reassigned to new projects.
Risk Management for Resources	The project will identify and manage risks related to resources, such as delays in procurement, team member availability, and issues with the new machines or software.

Table 17: Resource Management Plan from ChatGPT

6. 20 Create a RACI Chart: Using the following prompt

RACI CHART PROMPT

//Based on the information I have shared with you about this project, create for me a DETAILED

RACI Chart using dummy data.//

RACI CHART						
Task/Role	**Project Manager**	**IT Team**	**Quality Assurance Team**	**Procurement Team**	**CIO**	**Mayor's Office**
Define Project Scope	A	R	C	C	I	I
Procure Machines	C	R	I	A	C	I
Software Installation	C	A	R	I	C	I
Troubleshooting	C	A	C	I	C	I
Quality Auditing	C	I	A	I	C	C
Communicate with Stakeholders	A	I	I	I	C	R
Risk Management	A	C	C	C	R	I

Table 18: RACI Chart from ChatGPT

6. 21 Create a Communications Management Plan: Using the following prompt

COMMUNICATIONS MANAGEMENT PLAN PROMPT

//Based on the information I have shared with you about this project, create for me a DETAILED
Communications Management Plan using dummy data.//

COMMUNICATIONS MANAGEMENT PLAN	
Section	**Description**
Communication Goals	Ensure all stakeholders are informed of project updates, changes, and milestones. Foster an environment of transparency and open communication.
Stakeholders & Communication Needs	Key stakeholders include the CIO, local workers, and the Mayor's office. The CIO will need regular project updates, local workers need to be informed of software changes, and the Mayor's office requires status reports for governance purposes.
Communication Methods	Emails for regular updates, in-person meetings for in-depth discussions, and video conferencing for remote communication.
Frequency of Communication	Weekly status reports via email. Daily stand-up meetings for the project team. Monthly meetings with the CIO and Mayor's office. Ad hoc meetings as necessary.
Responsibility for Communication	The Project Manager is responsible for most communication. The IT Team will communicate technical issues, the Quality Assurance Team will report on quality checks, and the Procurement Team will update on procurement status.
Communication Standards & Processes	All communications should be clear, concise, and professional. Emails should follow a standard format and meetings should have a set agenda distributed in advance.
Escalation Process	Any issues that cannot be resolved within the team should be escalated to the Project Manager. If the Project Manager cannot resolve the issue, it should be escalated to the CIO.
Documentation Storage/Access	All project documentation will be stored on a secure cloud server. Access will be granted based on job function and necessity.
Revision Process	The Communications Management Plan will be reviewed monthly and updated as needed. Any changes will be communicated to the team.

Table 19: Communications Management Plan from ChatGPT

6. 22 Create a Risk Management Plan: Using the following prompt

RISK MANAGEMENT PLAN PROMPT

//Based on the information I have shared with you about this project, create for me a DETAILED

Risk Management Plan using dummy data.//

RISK MANAGEMENT PLAN	
Section	**Description**
Risk Management Goals	To identify, assess, and manage potential risks that could hinder project objectives or timelines.
Risk Identification	The team will identify risks through brainstorming sessions, SWOT analysis, and expert judgement. Risks will be documented in a risk register.
Risk Assessment	Each identified risk will be assessed for probability and impact on a scale of 1 (low) to 5 (high). This will be conducted by the Project Manager and relevant team members.
Risk Response Planning	For each risk, a response strategy (Avoid, Transfer, Mitigate, Accept) will be chosen based on the risk's probability and impact. Contingency plans will also be developed for high-impact risks.
Roles and Responsibilities	The Project Manager is responsible for overseeing risk management activities. However, all team members are responsible for identifying and reporting potential risks.
Risk Tracking and Reporting	The risk register will be updated regularly and reviewed in weekly team meetings. If a risk event occurs, it will be reported to all relevant stakeholders.
Budgeting for Risk Management	A contingency reserve will be established in the project budget to address risks that become issues.
Risk Management Process Review	The effectiveness of risk responses and the risk management process as a whole will be reviewed periodically and after major risk events.

Table 20: Risk Management Plan from ChatGPT

6. 23 Create a Risk Register: Using the following prompt

RISK REGISTER PROMPT

//Based on the information I have shared with you about this project, create for me a DETAILED Risk Register using dummy data.//

RISK REGISTER							
Risk ID	Risk Event	Probability	Impact	Risk Score	Risk Response	Risk Owner	Status
R1	Software incompatibility with existing systems	3	4	12	Mitigate	IT Lead	Open
R2	Delays in software delivery	2	4	8	Transfer	Procurement Manager	Open
R3	Insufficient training leading to improper use of software	4	3	12	Mitigate	Training Coordinator	Open
R4	Resistance to change from local workers	3	3	9	Mitigate	Change Management Specialist	Open
R5	Budget overrun due to unexpected costs	2	4	8	Avoid	Project Manager	Open
R6	Data loss during software transition	2	5	10	Avoid	IT Lead	Open

Table 21: Risk Register from ChatGPT

6. 24 Create a Procurement Management Plan: Using the following prompt

PROCUREMENT MANAGEMENT PLAN PROMPT
//Based on the information I have shared with you about this project, create for me a DETAILED Procurement Management Plan using dummy data.//

PROCUREMENT MANAGEMENT PLAN	
Section	**Description**
Plan Overview	This Procurement Management Plan outlines the process for acquiring necessary goods and services for the project. It covers procurement strategy, contract management, risk mitigation, and supplier selection.
Roles & Responsibilities	The Project Manager is responsible for overseeing the procurement process. The Procurement Officer is responsible for supplier communication, contract negotiations, and purchase management.
Procurement Strategy	The strategy is competitive bidding. It allows for the selection of the supplier offering the best value in terms of quality, price, and delivery time.
Supplier Selection Criteria	Suppliers will be evaluated based on their track record, financial stability, delivery schedule, price, and quality of goods/services.
Contract Type	Fixed price contracts will be used to ensure budget control.
Risk Management	Any risks associated with procurement (e.g., late delivery, poor quality, supplier insolvency) will be identified, assessed, and managed through the risk management process.
Performance Metrics	Supplier performance will be measured based on delivery time, quality of goods/services, and adherence to contract terms.
Change Management Process	Any changes to procurement requirements will go through a formal change control process, including impact assessment and approval.
Procurement Documentation	All procurement activities will be documented and stored centrally for audit purposes.

Table 22: Procurement Management Plan from ChatGPT

6. 25 Create an RFP: Using the following prompt

REQUEST FOR PROPOSAL (RFP) PROMPT

//Based on the information I have shared with you about this project, create for me a DETAILED RFP for this project for a part of the project that could be outsourced/contracted using dummy data.//

REQUEST FOR PROPOSAL
Project Title: Microsoft Office 365 Software Refresh Project
Project Manager: [Project Manager's Name]
Introduction and Executive Summary
The City of Phoenix is issuing an RFP to find a qualified supplier to provide training services for our IT department workers in the Motor Vehicle Division, who will be using Microsoft Office 365 after a software refresh.
Objectives
The objective of this RFP is to identify a vendor who can provide comprehensive training for 5000 employees, ensuring smooth transition and minimum downtime.
Scope of Work
The selected vendor will be required to develop and implement a comprehensive training program on Microsoft Office 365. The training should be a mix of online and offline modules and should cover all features of the software. The vendor is also expected to provide training materials and handouts.
Proposal Submission Guidelines
Proposals should be submitted via email to [email address] by [date and time]. Proposals should include a detailed outline of the training plan, cost proposal, company profile, and references.
Evaluation Criteria
Proposals will be evaluated based on the following criteria:
Vendor's experience in providing similar services
Quality and comprehensiveness of the training plan
Cost-effectiveness of the proposal
References
Terms and Conditions
The selected vendor will be expected to sign a contract outlining the terms and conditions of the engagement, including confidentiality, payment terms, and termination clause.
Contact Information
For any queries related to this RFP, please contact [Project Manager's Name] at [email address or phone number].
This RFP invites prospective vendors to submit their proposal outlining their qualifications, proposed approach, and costs. It provides a fair and transparent process for selecting a vendor who can best meet our project's training needs.

Table 23: Request for Proposal (RFP) from ChatGPT

6. 26 Create a Sample Contract/Agreement: Using the following prompt

CONTRACT/AGREEMENT PROMPT

//Based on the information I have shared with you about this project, create for me a DETAILED

contract/agreement with a vendor or supplier using dummy data.//

Agreement for Training Services
Parties Involved:
The City of Phoenix, located at [address] (hereafter referred to as the "Client").
[Vendor's Name], located at [address] (hereafter referred to as the "Vendor").
1. Scope of Services
The Vendor agrees to provide comprehensive training services for 5000 employees of the Client's IT department workers in the Motor Vehicle Division on the Microsoft Office 365 software, as per the requirements detailed in Exhibit A, attached hereto.
2. Payment Terms
The Client agrees to pay the Vendor the amount of [amount in USD], as detailed in Exhibit B, attached hereto. Payment will be made in [number] installments after the completion of each training module.
3. Term and Termination
This agreement will commence on [start date] and will continue until [end date] unless otherwise terminated by either party with [number] days' notice.
4. Confidentiality
The Vendor agrees to maintain the confidentiality of all proprietary information it may have access to during the course of this engagement.
5. Liability and Indemnification
The Vendor will be responsible for any damage or loss caused due to their negligence or failure to adhere to the terms of this agreement. The Vendor will indemnify and hold the Client harmless from any claims arising out of its services.
6. Governing Law
This agreement shall be governed by and interpreted in accordance with the laws of the state of Arizona.
7. Signatures
By signing below, both parties agree to adhere to all terms and conditions outlined in this agreement.
The City of Phoenix
[Signature]
[Printed Name and Title]
[Date]
[Vendor's Name]
[Signature]
[Printed Name and Title]
[Date]

Table 24:Contractual Agreement from ChatGPT

6. 27 Create a Stakeholder Register: Using the following prompt

STAKEHOLDER REGISTER

//Based on the information I have shared with you about this project, create for me a DETAILED Stakeholder Register using dummy data.//

STAKEHOLDER REGISTER					
Stakeholder Name	**Role**	**Contact Information**	**Influence**	**Expectations**	**Communication Preferences**
John Doe (CIO)	Approves key decisions	john.doe@email.com, Ext. 1234	High	Timely and successful completion of the project	Prefers weekly updates via email
Jane Smith (IT Department)	End-user	jane.smith@email.com, Ext. 2345	Medium	Proper training on the new software	Prefers face-to-face communication
Vendor's IT Department	Project execution	vendor@email.com	High	Timely payments and clear instructions	Prefers communication via regular conference calls
Mayor's Office	Project oversight	mayorsoffice@email.com	High	Completion of project with minimal public disruption	Prefers monthly updates via formal reports
Local Workers	Affected by project	localworkers@email.com	Low	Transparency about changes	Prefers updates via townhall meetings and newsletters
Power Users	Initial feedback providers	powerusers@email.com	High	Inclusion in the decision-making process	Prefers direct and frequent communication

Table 25:Contractual Agreement from ChatGPT

6. 28 Create a Stakeholder Engagement Plan: Using the following prompt

STAKEHOLDER ENGAGEMENT PLAN PROMPT

//Based on the information I have shared with you about this project, create for me a DETAILED Stakeholder Engagement Plan using dummy data.//

Stakeholder Engagement Plan				
Project Name: Microsoft Office 365 Software Refresh Project for the City of Phoenix				
Project Manager: [Project Manager's Name]				
Stakeholder	**Role in Project**	**Current Engagement Level**	**Desired Engagement Level**	**Communication Plan**
Chief Information Officer (CIO)	Approves key decisions	Low	High	Weekly project status reports; Monthly project review meetings
IT Department workers in the Motor Vehicle Division	End-users of the new software	Medium	High	Daily stand-up meetings; Training sessions
Vendor's IT Department	Responsible for deployment and troubleshooting	High	High	Regular communication on progress, issues, and concerns
Mayor's Office	Provides overall project oversight and support	Low	Medium	Monthly project updates
Local Workers	Affected by the changes in the software	Low	Medium	Regular project updates through email; Townhall meetings
Power Users	Assist in software testing and initial feedback	Medium	High	Frequent interaction during testing phases

Table 26:Stakeholder Engagement Plan   from ChatGPT

6. 29 Create a Project Report for a Project: Using the following prompt

WORK PERFORMANCE REPORT PROMPT

//Based on the information I have shared with you about this project, create for me a DETAILED Project Work Performance Report using dummy data. Show the project as being ahead of schedule and under budget. //

Project Work Performance Report
Project Name: Microsoft Office 365 Software Refresh Project for the City of Phoenix
Project Manager: [Project Manager's Name]
Project Status: As of [Current Date]
Schedule Performance:
Scheduled Completion Date: February 2024
Estimated Completion Date: December 2023
Status: Ahead of Schedule
Cost Performance:
Total Budgeted Cost: $500,000
Actual Cost to Date: $200,000
Projected Final Cost: $475,000
Status: Under Budget
Key Achievements:
Successful installation of Office 365 software in 2000 out of 5000 machines ahead of the planned schedule.
Procurement of machines for software refresh was done under the budget due to the negotiation of bulk purchase discounts from the vendor.
Issues and Concerns:
None at this moment due to effective project management and stakeholder engagement.
Risk Management:
No new risks identified. All previously identified risks are being monitored and managed as per the Risk Management Plan.
Next Steps:
Continue with the deployment of Office 365 software in the remaining machines.
Begin training sessions for IT department workers in the Motor Vehicle Division.
This Project Work Performance Report should be used as a tool for understanding the project's progress and status. It's a testament to effective planning and execution, as shown by the project being ahead of schedule and under budget. The team will continue to monitor and manage the project to ensure it remains on this successful path.

Table 27:Work Performance Report from ChatGPT

6. 30 Create an Issue Log: Using the following prompt

ISSUE LOG PROMPT

//Based on the information I have shared with you about this project, create for me a DETAILED

Issue Log using dummy data.//

ISSUE LOG							
Issue ID	**Issue Description**	**Date Identified**	**Raised By**	**Impact**	**Current Status**	**Resolution Date**	**Assigned To**
IL-001	Delay in shipment of 500 machines from the vendor	7/1/2023	Jane Smith, IT Department	Medium	Resolved	7/10/2023	John Doe, CIO
IL-002	Office 365 software installation issues in 50 machines	7/15/2023	Vendor's IT Department	High	Resolved	7/25/2023	Vendor's IT Department
IL-003	Concerns from local workers about software transition	8/1/2023	Local Workers	Low	In Progress	Expected 08/15/2023	Project Manager
IL-004	Training material not ready for IT department workers	8/10/2023	Jane Smith, IT Department	Medium	Open	Expected 08/20/2023	Training

Table 28:Issue Log from ChatGPT

6. 31 Create a Risk Report: Using the following prompt

RISK REPORT PROMPT

//Based on the information I have shared with you about this project, create for me a DETAILED Risk Report using dummy data. Include both threat and opportunity highlights and overall project risk and risk exposure the best way possible.//

Risk Report										
Project Name: Microsoft Office 365 Software Refresh Project for the City of Phoenix										
Project Manager: [Project Manager's Name]										
Project Risk Score: Moderate Risk (35/70)										
Current Risk Exposure: $120,000										
Risk Summary: The project's moderate risk score is a reflection of the balance between high-impact technical risks (compatibility issues, software installa										
Risk Highlights:										
Risk ID	**Risk Description**	**Risk Category**	**Risk Type**	**Probability**	**Impact**	**Priority**	**Current Status**	**Response Strategy**	**Mitigation Actions**	**Responsible Party**
RR-001	Delay in delivery of machines due to supply chain issues	Procurement	Threat	Medium	High	High	Monitored	Mitigation	Secured multiple vendors for procurement	Procurement Manager
RR-002	Compatibility issues with existing IT infrastructure	Technical	Threat	Low	High	Medium	Resolved	Mitigation	Completed infrastructure readiness assessment before software installation	IT Team
RR-003	Resistance from local workers to transition to new software	People	Threat	High	Medium	High	Active	Acceptance	Implement a comprehensive change management strategy including proper communication and training	Change Management Team
RR-004	Software installation errors causing work disruption	Technical	Threat	Medium	High	High	Active	Mitigation	Enlist vendor support for software installation; conduct installation during non-peak hours	IT Team
RR-005	Budget overrun due to unforeseen costs	Financial	Threat	Low	High	Medium	Monitored	Mitigation	Rigorous budget planning and tracking; secured contingency budget	Project Manager
Key Opportunities:										
Opportunity RR-006 aims to exploit the potential for improved productivity due to the capabilities of Microsoft Office 365, leading to improved workflow efficiency. RR-007 outlines the opportunity to reduce operating costs by exploiting the benefits of cloud-based solutions.										
Key Threats:										
Threat RR-001 addresses the potential delay in machine delivery due to supply chain issues. RR-002 and RR-004 represent technical risks associated with compatibility and software installation errors, respectively.										
This Risk Report is used to identify, categorize, prioritize, and manage potential project risks. Active monitoring and implementation of appropriate response strategies help ensure project success despite these uncertainties. The report will be updated as new risks emerge and existing ones are resolved.										

Table 29:Risk Report from ChatGPT

6. 32 Create a Lessons Learned Register: Using the following prompt

LESSONS LEARNED REGISTER PROMPT

//Based on the information I have shared with you about this project, create for me a DETAILED Lessons Learned Register. Include as much relevant information as possible.//

ID	Lesson Description	Category	Impact on the Project	Recommended Actions	Responsible Party
LESSONS LEARNED REGISTER					
LL-001	Securing multiple vendors for procurement reduced the risk of machine delivery delay	Procurement	Positive	Future projects should consider securing multiple vendors to reduce dependency and delay risks	Procurement Manager
LL-002	Completing an infrastructure readiness assessment prior to software installation minimized compatibility issues	Technical	Positive	Incorporate infrastructure readiness assessments in future projects to anticipate potential compatibility issues	IT Team
LL-003	Resistance from workers was effectively managed through a comprehensive change management strategy	People	Positive	Reinforce the use of change management strategies including proper communication and training in future projects	Change Management Team
LL-004	Software installation during non-peak hours reduced work disruption	Technical	Positive	Continue to schedule major IT changes during non-peak hours to minimize work disruption	IT Team
LL-005	Rigorous budget planning and tracking helped to manage unforeseen costs	Financial	Positive	Encourage detailed budget planning and tracking in future projects. Secure a contingency budget for managing risks	Project Manager
LL-006	Productivity improved significantly with comprehensive training sessions on utilizing Microsoft Office 365's full potential	Operational	Positive	Ensure future projects involving new tools or software include detailed training sessions for end users	Training Team

Table 30:Lessons Learned Register from ChatGPT

6. 33 Create a Project Management Plan: Using the following prompt

PROJECT MANAGEMENT PLAN PROMPT

//Based on the information I have shared with you about this project, create for me a Project Management Plan in tabular view. Include as much information as possible.//

PROJECT MANAGEMENT PLAN LITE	
Section	**Description**
Project Overview	The project aims to execute a software refresh for the City of Phoenix, targeting the IT department workers in the Motor Vehicle Division. The duration of the project spans from June 2023 to February 2024.
Scope Management Plan	Describes the process of scope definition, validation, and control. It includes details about how the scope will be defined, developed, monitored, controlled, and validated.
Schedule Management Plan	Describes the methodology and tools used to create, manage, and control the project schedule. It also includes estimated project durations and a timeline.
Cost Management Plan	Defines how the project costs will be estimated, budgeted, managed, monitored, and controlled.
Quality Management Plan	Describes how the project team will implement the organization's quality policy. It outlines quality control and quality management activities.
Resource Management Plan	Describes how to estimate, acquire, manage, and utilize physical and team resources.
Communications Management Plan	Identifies and organizes communication methods for the duration of the project. It specifies the information to be communicated, who will receive it, who will send it, and the frequency of communication.
Risk Management Plan	Outlines the approach to identifying and managing risks throughout the project. It includes risk identification, risk analysis, risk response planning, and risk monitoring and control.
Procurement Management Plan	Details the procurement of necessary resources, the type of contract to be used, the risks involved, and the metrics for measuring supplier performance.
Stakeholder Engagement Plan	Identifies strategies to effectively engage stakeholders in project decisions and execution based on their needs, expectations, and impact on the project.

Table 31: Project Management Plan Lite from ChatGPT

6. 34 Create a Final Report: Using the following prompt

FINAL REPORT PROMPT

//Based on the information I have shared with you about this project, create for me a Final Report in tabular view. Include as much information as possible.//

FINAL REPORT	
Section	**Description**
Project Overview	The project aimed to execute a software refresh for the City of Phoenix, targeting the IT department workers in the Motor Vehicle Division. The project started in June 2023 and was successfully completed in February 2024.
Objectives and Scope	The objective of the project was to procure and deploy 5000 machines for the software refresh. The scope included all IT department workers in the Motor Vehicle Division.
Performance Analysis	The project was completed ahead of schedule and under budget, achieving all defined success criteria. The Cost Performance Index (CPI) was [value] and the Schedule Performance Index (SPI) was [value], indicating efficient cost and time management.
Deliverables Status	All project deliverables were successfully completed and accepted. The deliverables met the required standards and fulfilled the defined scope.
Resource Utilization	The project made optimal use of the resources provided by the vendors' IT department. The resources were allocated and managed efficiently, with no major issues or bottlenecks.
Stakeholder Satisfaction	The stakeholders, including the CIO, other local workers, and the Mayor's office, expressed satisfaction with the project's execution and results. Regular communication and updates ensured stakeholder engagement throughout the project.
Risk Management	Identified risks were effectively managed through proactive risk response strategies. No major risks materialized during the project.
Quality Management	Quality audits showed that the project adhered to the quality standards set out in the Quality Management Plan. Any defects identified were promptly addressed and corrected.
Lessons Learned	A lessons learned register has been created to capture insights and experiences from this project. This register will be used to inform and improve future projects.
Project Closure	The project was formally closed following confirmation of completed deliverables, stakeholder acceptance, and settlement of all financial obligations.

Table 32: Final Report from ChatGPT

6. 35 Respond to an angry customer or stakeholder: Using the following prompt

STAKEHOLDER COMMUNICATION & ENGAGEMENT PROMPT

//Based on the information I have shared with you about this SITUATION (CUSTOMER IS ANGRY ABOUT MISSED DEADLINE, DUE TO SUPPLIER ISSUE), create for me, a response to re-engage customer trust while demonstrating empathy. SUPPLIER HAS BEEN ASKED TO EXPEDITE. Will do everything possible to get back on schedule.//

Subject: Addressing Your Recent Concerns and Our Path Forward

Dear [Customer's Name],

I hope this message finds you well. I'm reaching out to address the recent issue we've encountered regarding the missed deadline. First and foremost, I would like to express my deepest regret for this unforeseen situation and any inconvenience it may have caused you.

I completely understand your disappointment, and I empathize with your position. We strive to uphold the highest standards of service, and in this instance, we fell short. Please know that we take this matter very seriously.

The delay, caused by an unexpected issue with our supplier, is not characteristic of our usual business practice. We have already engaged with the supplier and are making every effort to expedite the process. The aim is to remedy the delay as swiftly as possible and get back on schedule without compromising the quality of the end product.

In the meantime, we are implementing immediate actions to ensure greater efficiency in our processes to prevent such incidents from reoccurring. We will keep you updated on our progress and make sure that moving forward, we deliver on our commitments in a timely manner.

I want to assure you that your satisfaction and trust are paramount to us. Our relationship with you is something we value greatly, and we are committed to restoring and maintaining your trust in our service.

Once again, I apologize for this situation and appreciate your patience and understanding as we navigate through this. Please feel free to reach out to me directly if you wish to discuss this further or if there's anything else you need.

Thank you for your understanding.

Best Regards,

[Your Name] [Your Position]

6. 36 Generate ideas of how to tackle problems or issues: Using the following prompt

> **CONFLICT RESOLUTION IDEAS**
>
> **//Based on the information I have shared with you about this SITUATION (TEAM MEMBER JAKE IS MAD AND JEALOUS OVER PROMOTION OF TEAM MEMBER JULIA AND WANTS TO LEAVE THE TEAM), generate ideas on how to resolve this situation.//**

OUTPUT: Navigating conflict within a team requires a tactful approach. It's essential to foster an environment where everyone feels heard, valued, and understood. Here are some steps you could consider in this situation:

1. One-on-One Discussion with Jake: Start with a private conversation with Jake to understand his feelings and concerns. This will help to validate his emotions and ensure he feels heard.

2. Clear Communication: Clearly communicate the basis for the promotion decision. This isn't about comparing Jake and Julia, but rather about making sure Jake understands the process and criteria that led to Julia's promotion. Explain how the decision was made, keeping in mind confidentiality and respect for both parties.

3. Goal Setting and Skill Development: Work with Jake to set new goals and create a clear plan for skill development. This will help him understand the steps needed for his own advancement.

4. Foster Peer Recognition: Encourage a culture where team members regularly recognize each other's efforts and accomplishments. This will help Jake feel more appreciated and might ease his feelings of jealousy.

5. Promote Team Unity: Consider team-building activities to foster stronger relationships and ease tension within the team. This can improve the overall team dynamic and promote a more positive work environment.

6. Offer Mentorship: If possible, offer Jake a mentor within the organization who can provide guidance, help him navigate his feelings, and provide perspective on career progression.

7. Continuous Feedback and Communication: Maintain open lines of communication and provide continuous feedback to Jake about his performance, potential areas for growth, and future opportunities.

8. Constructive Resolution: If Jake still wants to leave the team, it's important to handle it constructively. If feasible, offer him alternatives within the organization where he could feel more comfortable and see a clear path for progression.

Remember, it's crucial to ensure that Jake's feelings are validated and that any feelings of resentment are addressed promptly to avoid long-term impact on the team's morale and productivity.

Conclusion

While we've dedicated substantial effort to generating these project artifacts, it's crucial to remember that their existence alone doesn't guarantee project success. Despite possessing a comprehensive array of well-crafted documents, projects can still falter without effective stakeholder engagement and communication. The tools and processes we've covered are integral to project management, but they don't supersede the importance of human interaction and collaboration.

Remember, AI like ChatGPT is a powerful tool that can enhance your project management processes, but it can't replace a project manager's critical thinking, leadership, and decision-making skills. The power of AI is best harnessed when used as an adjunct, assisting you in organizing, planning, and documenting your project. However, it can't foresee every nuance, engage with stakeholders, or handle complex decision-making processes; this is where your indispensable role as a human project manager comes into play.

While leveraging AI can provide a competitive advantage, it's your ability to lead, communicate effectively, and manage the various complexities of the project that will ultimately drive its success. So view AI not as your leader but as a strategic partner that complements your skill set and helps to enhance your project management capabilities.

To wrap up, utilizing AI such as ChatGPT in project management represents an innovative approach to tackling complex tasks and enhancing productivity. By automating various aspects of project documentation, AI can free up human bandwidth, enabling project managers to focus more on strategic decision-making, stakeholder engagement, and team leadership.

However, it's vital to remember that AI is a tool, not a replacement for human judgment and expertise. It cannot understand the nuances of interpersonal relationships or manage dynamic changes in project requirements the way a human can. Despite AI's remarkable capacity to generate detailed project artifacts, it's still up to the human project manager to interpret these outputs, apply them to real-world scenarios, and adjust them to align with the project's evolving circumstances.

In essence, the marriage of AI and human intelligence in project management represents a promising frontier in the field. When applied correctly, AI can assist in reducing manual labor, streamlining workflows, and increasing overall efficiency. Nevertheless, the irreplaceable value of human insight, intuition, and leadership remain at the core of successful project management. This blend of AI assistance and human leadership is the key to navigating the ever-evolving landscape of project management effectively.

It's essential to remember that AI, while impressive in its capabilities, has its limitations. AI cannot substitute the human touch required in project management. It can't attend meetings, send meeting invitations, engage with stakeholders, or understand the subtleties of team dynamics. AI can't interpret nonverbal cues, gauge emotional responses, or preemptively manage interpersonal conflicts.

As a project manager, these critical tasks fall under your jurisdiction. AI might assist in producing detailed project artifacts and streamline certain problem-solving tasks, but it can't replace your ability to foster relationships, inspire trust, and facilitate effective communication. Understanding these strengths and limitations will enable you to use AI as a tool to augment your skills rather than as a substitute for your expertise. Your strategic insight, empathetic leadership, and interpersonal skills remain crucial to the success of any project management endeavor.

CHAPTER SEVEN: AGILE PROJECT MANAGEMENT AND AI INTEGRATION

> *"To truly embrace Agile, one must dance with change and partner with innovation. AI is not just a tool; it's the rhythm that enhances our agility, propelling us towards a future of infinite possibilities."*

As the echoes of laughter from the previous chapter's antics subsided, Phill, ever the consummate professional, adjusted his jazzy tie, polished his gleaming PMP lapel pin, and refocused his class's attention on the upcoming topic.

"Let's revisit Agile project management principles," Phill started, launching the first slide of the day. There was a collective groan from the back of the room – Phill knew his jesters were never keen on revisiting topics.

"Hey, Phill, can we have an AI-powered Agile class instead?" quipped Kevin, earning a round of giggles from the class. "That's the spirit, Kevin!" Phill retorted, laughing along with his students. "But remember, to leverage AI effectively, we need to first understand Agile principles thoroughly." With a click of a button, on came the projector.

7.1 Understanding Agile Project Management Principle

Agile project management is a set of principles and practices that emphasizes iterative and incremental development, collaboration, and responding to change. Agile projects are typically broken down into smaller, more manageable tasks, and progress is tracked throughout the development process.

Some of the key principles of agile project management include:

- Customer collaboration: Agile teams work closely with their customers to ensure that the final product meets their needs.

- Iterative development: Agile projects are developed in short, iterative cycles, with each cycle resulting in a working product.

- Incremental delivery: Agile projects are delivered in increments, with each increment providing additional functionality.

- Responding to change: Agile teams are able to adapt to change quickly and easily.

Switching gears to "AI-Enabled Agile Project Planning," Phill spoke about the application of AI in enhancing Agile planning. He talked about how AI could analyze project data and suggest the most efficient way of organizing tasks, prioritizing work, and predicting potential roadblocks. Joey, always ready with a quip, wondered if AI could help plan his weekend. Phill smiled and remarked, "Joey, if your weekend is as complex as a project, AI might indeed come in handy! Now let's review the next slide!"

7.2 AI-Enabled Agile Project Planning

Artificial intelligence (AI) can be used to improve the efficiency and effectiveness of agile project planning. For example, AI can be used to:

- Automate repetitive tasks: AI can be used to automate tasks such as task tracking, risk assessment, and resource allocation based on data or spreadsheets fed into the system. This can free up team members to focus on more strategic tasks.

- Provide insights: AI can be used to analyze data and provide insights that can help teams make better decisions. For example, AI can be used to predict which tasks are most likely to be completed on time and within budget.

- Generate recommendations: AI can be used to generate recommendations for tasks, resources, and priorities. This can help teams to make more informed decisions about how to allocate their resources.

The ability to generate value in an Agile environment often hinges on the team's ability to ask the right questions and leverage available resources effectively. This is especially true when working on innovative projects where there may be no prior benchmarks or guidelines to follow.

Integrating AI in such scenarios can be a game-changer, acting as a rich source of information and insights, and enabling teams to approach problems from unique and data-driven perspectives.

Consider a simple prompt like, "How might we enhance user engagement for our new app?" In a traditional setting, team members would rely on their individual expertise and past experiences to brainstorm ideas. While this method has its merits, it could potentially limit the scope of ideas, as they're inherently tied to the team's existing knowledge.

However, by leveraging AI, the team could generate a broader range of innovative solutions. AI can analyze vast amounts of data, identify patterns, and provide relevant insights, helping teams to think outside their existing frameworks. For example, the AI could draw on data from successful apps in different industries, user behavior studies, and emerging tech trends to suggest unique engagement strategies that the team may not have considered.

Additionally, AI can streamline the brainstorming process. Instead of each team member suggesting ideas individually, they could all interact with the AI tool simultaneously, feeding their ideas into the system and getting instant feedback.

This could foster a more collaborative and dynamic brainstorming session, with AI providing real-time insights and stimulating further idea generation.

In essence, a simple AI-powered prompt can effectively drive idea generation in an Agile environment, thereby leading to more innovative solutions, improved productivity, and ultimately, superior project outcomes. It's about turning the unknown into a space for opportunity, and AI offers a valuable tool for doing just that.

In the forthcoming example, we will study how ChatGPT skillfully reacts to a spontaneous prompt I conceived for a novel holographic watch product. Observe the stark contrast between the succinctness of the initial prompt and the comprehensive output produced. Even in the face of my rudimentary and unpolished prompt, Chad GPT adeptly interprets the essence of my query and crafts an extensive product backlog for this pioneering product. This aptly illustrates how AI can bridge the gap between a rough concept and a fleshed-out plan, a testament to its transformative potential in project management.

7.2.1 Generate a Product Backlog for a New Innovative Product: Using the following prompt

INNOVATION IDEAS FOR A NEW HOLOGRAPHIC WATCH (HOLOGRAM GENERATOR)

//MY TEAM IS WORKING ON A NEW PROJECT AND THE PRODUCT IS A WORN DEVICE LIKE A WATCH TO PROJECT HOLOGRAM IMAGES DURING MEETINGS WHICH WOULD TAKE THE INPUT OF EACH ATTENDEE'S CAMERA AND MAKE IT LOOK AS IF WE WERE ALL SEATED ON A ROUND TABLE EACH USER SHOULD BE ABLE TO PROJECT THE SAME HOLOGRAPHIC IMAGE AT THEIR LOCATION TO GET A FEEL THAT WE ARE ALL IN THE SAME PLACE. CREATE A PRODUCT BACKLOG FOR THIS PROJECT.//

OUTPUT

Product backlog creation is a key step in defining the scope and goals for a project. The following is an example of a backlog for the Holographic Watch Project:

1. **Project Initialization:**

   - Market research and analysis
   - Define project goals and key performance indicators (KPIs)
   - Assemble project team and define roles/responsibilities

2. **Hardware Development:**

   - Develop watch design specifications
   - Prototype watch design
   - Integrate hologram projection technology
   - Optimize energy usage and battery life
   - Test hardware durability and reliability

3. **Software Development:**

   - Develop software to capture and convert video input into holographic output
   - Implement user interface for watch controls
   - Develop software to synchronize multiple devices
   - Integrate software with existing video conferencing platforms
   - Optimize software for different operating systems and devices

4. **User Experience (UX):**

   - Design intuitive interface for watch and holographic controls
   - Prototype and test user interface
   - Integrate user feedback into UX design
   - Design and test accessibility features

5. **Holographic Experience Development:**
   - Define specifications for holographic projection (resolution, brightness, colors, etc.)
   - Test different projection surfaces/environments
   - Optimize holographic display for clarity and realism
   - Develop functionality for 360-degree view

6. **Security & Privacy:**
   - Develop encryption standards for video conferencing
   - Create privacy policy and user agreements
   - Implement user controls for privacy settings

7. **Testing and Quality Assurance (QA):**
   - Develop testing protocols for hardware, software, and UX
   - Perform comprehensive system testing
   - Address any bugs or issues found during testing
   - Implement changes based on user feedback

8. **Marketing and Launch:**
   - Develop marketing and launch plan
   - Implement pre-launch activities (press releases, teasers, etc.)
   - Coordinate product launch
   - Post-launch customer support and maintenance

Remember, an effective backlog is a living document. It should be regularly reviewed, refined, and reprioritized as needed throughout the project. This is merely a starting point!

As a vast language model, ChatGPT has the unique ability to take even your most formative ideas, grasp the core concept, draw upon its extensive knowledge base, and generate concise, coherent, and logically sound responses in the majority of cases. However, it's important to remember that the tool's efficacy is not absolute. There may be occasions where you need to refine, adjust, and optimize your prompts to elicit the most valuable and relevant responses. In essence, effective interaction with ChatGPT is an art that balances the clarity of your query with the model's impressive capabilities.

"Leveraging AI for Agile Communication and Collaboration" was the next slide. Phill explained the use of AI in streamlining communication, managing teams, and fostering collaboration in an Agile environment. He highlighted AI tools that assist in coordinating distributed teams, automating updates, and facilitating real-time decision-making.

The usually raucous Kevin asked earnestly if AI could prevent misunderstandings in his group project. Phill commended the thoughtful question, responding that while AI might not eliminate all human errors, it could indeed provide clarity and help keep everyone on the same page, thereby reducing potential misunderstandings. "Now let's cover a few more points!" Phill exclaimed pointing at the screen.

7.3 Leveraging AI for Agile Communication and Collaboration

AI can also be used to improve agile communication and collaboration. For example, AI can be used to:

- Translate languages: AI can be used to translate documents and conversations between different languages. This can help teams to communicate more effectively with each other, even if those communicating do not speak the same language.

- Summarize text: AI can be used to summarize text documents. This can help teams to quickly and easily understand the key points of a document. ChatGPT is exceptional at this!

- Generate reports: AI can be used to generate reports on project progress. This can help teams to track their progress and identify any potential problems.

Lastly, Phill announced the exercise: "Integrating AI into Agile Project Management Practices." The jesters groaned while the studious ones were already brainstorming.

7.4 Exercise: Integrating AI into Agile Project Management Practices

Here is an exercise that you can try to integrate AI into agile project management practices:

- Identify a specific agile project that you are working on.
- Think about how AI could be used to improve the efficiency or effectiveness of the project.
- Research different AI tools and technologies that could be used for the project.
- Create a plan for how you would integrate AI into the project.
- Implement the plan and evaluate the results.

This is just one example of how AI can be used to improve agile project management practices. There are many other ways that AI can be used, and the specific approach that you take will depend on the specific project and the specific needs of the team.

As the class wrapped up, Phill sat back, satisfied with another successful, lively session. The classroom chatter gradually faded, but Phill's jazzy suit, eccentric ties, and shiny PMP lapel pin would continue to spark animated conversations and learning, just as they had today.

CHAPTER EIGHT: AI IN HYBRID PROJECT MANAGEMENT

"

"Refusing to consider hybrid solutions is not being AGILE!"

As the laughter from Kevin's latest quip faded, Phill straightened his flamboyant tie, a stark contrast to his otherwise professional attire. He cleared his throat and his eyes twinkled behind his glasses.

"Alright, scholars and jesters, it's time to switch gears," Phill announced, drawing the attention of the class. His hands worked deftly, bringing up the next slide deck on the projector. The title read ' Exploring Hybrid Project Management Approaches', and the room fell silent in anticipation.

`

"With the rapid evolution of project management methodologies," Phill began, "we're seeing a significant shift toward hybrid approaches. These methods, my dear students, blend the best of both predictive and agile worlds."

With that, he dove into the discussion, weaving an intricate tapestry of knowledge about hybrid project management and how he believed in hybrid project management being the way forward. "I believe in hybrid project management so much that I have bought the website www.hybridprojectmanagement.com!" He shared enthusiastically motioning to the slide beaming on the screen.

> **8.1 Exploring Hybrid Project Management Approaches**
>
> In this chapter, we journey into the concept of hybrid project management, which combines traditional predictive methodologies with agile approaches, and how artificial intelligence (AI) can enhance and support this hybrid approach. Hybrid project management recognizes that different projects require different management methodologies and that a one-size-fits-all approach may not be suitable. By combining the strengths of predictive and agile frameworks and practices, organizations can achieve a flexible and adaptable project management framework.
>
> - We begin by exploring various hybrid project management approaches. These approaches involve tailoring project management practices to suit the specific needs of each project, leveraging the best practices from predictive and agile methodologies. This customization ensures that project management processes are aligned with the unique characteristics, constraints, and requirements of the project at hand. We discuss the importance of evaluating project characteristics, stakeholder expectations, and organizational culture to determine the most suitable hybrid approach for a given project.

"Just when they thought they could relax," Phill continued, pointing towards Kevin and his gang of jesters, "it's time to revisit our old friends - Predictive and Agile methodologies. Only this time, we're exploring how they join forces in a hybrid environment." Phill navigated through the complexities of merging predictive planning with the adaptability of agile, drawing on real-world examples that brought the subject to life.

8.2 Combining Predictive and Agile Approaches

Next, we explore the integration of predictive and agile methodologies within hybrid project management. Predictive methodologies, such as the waterfall model, emphasize detailed planning, sequential execution, and a focus on documentation. Agile methodologies, on the other hand, prioritize flexibility, adaptability, iterative development, and collaboration.

We explore how organizations can combine the strengths of both approaches to create a hybrid project management approach. For example, predictive methodologies can be utilized during the initial planning and requirement gathering phase, while agile methodologies can be employed during the development and testing stages.

By adopting this approach, organizations can strike a balance between predictability and adaptability, reducing risks and increasing project success rates.

We also discuss how AI technologies can enhance the integration of predictive and agile methodologies. AI tools can assist in automating repetitive tasks, improving communication and collaboration, and providing real-time insights and analytics. This integration enables project managers to make informed decisions and manage projects more effectively.

AI can help you develop responsibility-assignment matrices and ideas for hybrid team integration. I call this a hybrid RAM. Let's examine ways to leverage AI in a hybrid structure.

Prompting for Ideas and Insights in a Hybrid Environment

Consider a situation in which you are in a hybrid environment and you are at a loss for ideas on how to effectively integrate the team and prevent them stepping on each other 's toes. In such cases you can develop a prompt that sources hybrid integration ideas from the AI tool such as ChatGPT.

PROMPT:

HYBRID PROJECT MANAGEMENT PROMPT

//The project involves a hybrid team of developers to code, using agile and a predictive team from the business to drive implementation across the business units. How should the team integrate ideas and synergize? We have four developers, three testers, one architect, a product owner, a scrum master, a sponsor on the side of the business, a program manager, a project manager, and several end users who are stakeholders.//

OUTPUT FROM CHATGPT

To integrate ideas and synergize effectively within the hybrid team, you can follow these steps:

1. Establish a collaborative culture: Foster an environment where team members from both the development and business sides feel comfortable sharing their ideas and opinions. Encourage open communication, active listening, and mutual respect.

2. Clearly define roles and responsibilities: Ensure that each team member understands their role and responsibilities within the project. This clarity helps avoid confusion and duplication of efforts. Make sure everyone understands the agile development process, including the roles of the product owner, scrum master, and team members.

3. Conduct regular cross-functional meetings: Schedule regular meetings involving all team members to discuss progress, challenges, and ideas. These meetings can include daily stand-ups, sprint planning, sprint reviews, and retrospectives. This helps to align everyone's understanding of the project goals and fosters collaboration.

4. Encourage active participation: Encourage all team members to actively participate in discussions and decision-making processes. Developers, testers, architects, and end users should provide input based on their expertise and domain knowledge. Create a safe space for sharing diverse perspectives.

5. Use agile ceremonies effectively: Leverage agile ceremonies such as sprint planning, backlog refinement, and sprint reviews to facilitate collaboration and gather feedback. Involve the business

stakeholders, product owner, and end users in these ceremonies to ensure alignment between development efforts and business objectives.

6. Establish a shared vision: Ensure that the entire team understands and aligns with the project's vision and goals. Regularly communicate the project's objectives and milestones to maintain focus and motivation.

7. Foster cross-team collaboration: Encourage collaboration and knowledge sharing among developers, testers, and architects. Promote cross-functional pairing and encourage individuals to work outside their immediate roles if it helps solve problems or improve overall project outcomes.

8. Leverage retrospectives: Conduct regular retrospectives to reflect on what is working well and identify areas for improvement. Include both development and business team members in these sessions to encourage a holistic evaluation of the project.

9. Empower the team: Give the team autonomy and authority to make decisions within their respective roles. Empower developers and testers to provide feedback on the feasibility of business requirements, and empower the business team to drive implementation decisions based on their domain knowledge.

10. Facilitate stakeholder engagement: Involve end users and other stakeholders in the development process through user feedback sessions, demos, and user acceptance testing. This helps ensure that the final product meets their needs and expectations.

11. Remember, successful integration and synergy require active collaboration, effective communication, and a shared understanding of project objectives. By following these steps, you can create a cohesive hybrid team that maximizes the strengths of both the development and business sides to drive successful implementation across the business units.

 Here, our main goal is to use the AI tool as a coach, mentor and guide for the work we are integrating using both agile and hybrid approaches. The advantage is that, as a large language model, it is capable of giving wholesome advice and insights.

"Remember our discussion about AI in predictive and agile project management?" Phill asked the class, with a knowing smile. "Now, let's consider how AI can aid decision-making in hybrid projects." He dived into a captivating discussion, unravelling the potentials of AI in balancing the fluidity of Agile with the structure of Predictive methodologies in a hybrid model.

> **8.3 AI-Assisted Decision Making in Hybrid Projects**
>
> AI-assisted decision making plays a crucial role in hybrid project management. We explore how AI can analyze large volumes of data, identify patterns, and generate valuable insights to support decision-making processes. AI algorithms can process historical project data, industry benchmarks, and other relevant information to provide recommendations on resource allocation, risk management strategies, and project scheduling.
>
> We discuss the benefits of leveraging AI in decision making, such as improved accuracy, reduced bias, and increased efficiency. However, we also highlight the importance of human expertise and judgment in interpreting AI-generated insights and making final decisions. AI should be viewed as a tool to augment human capabilities rather than replace them.

Guidelines for collaborating with AI

It's crucial to approach this project with a focus on collaboration and humanity. By combining the best of AI capabilities with the individual skills, knowledge, and creativity of the team members, we can create a harmonious and effective working environment. Here's how we can make this integration more human-centered:

1. Fostering Team Relationships: AI can be seen as a 'team member' who is always available for assistance. It is an asset that doesn't replace the human touch, but enhances it. It's crucial to encourage the team to interact with the AI tool as they would with a coach or mentor. This includes asking questions, seeking advice, and learning from the insights the AI provides.

2. Human-AI Collaboration: The AI tool should not be used in isolation, but rather as a component of the team's collaborative efforts. Encourage team members to share their insights, learnings, and feedback from their interaction with the AI tool, which can foster a sense of community and shared understanding.

3. Respecting Human Skills: Remember to value the unique skills and capabilities that human team members bring to the project. This includes problem-solving, creativity, and empathy.

While the AI tool can provide insights and support decision-making, it is the human team members who will ultimately drive the project forward with their skills and abilities.

4. Emphasizing Continuous Learning: Using an AI tool can be a great learning opportunity for the team. It's important to foster a culture of continuous learning and curiosity. The AI can provide resources, tutorials, and case studies to help team members learn more about agile methodologies, project management techniques, and other relevant topics.

5. Balancing AI Advice with Human Judgment: While the AI tool can provide valuable advice and insights, it's essential to remember that these should be balanced with human judgment. Encourage team members to critically analyze the suggestions made by the AI tool, considering them as one of many resources in decision-making processes.

6. Human-centered Design: Use the AI tool to facilitate a human-centered design approach. It can provide data and insights about end users, stakeholders, and other human aspects of the project. This information can inform design decisions and help ensure that the project outcomes meet human needs and expectations.

Our goal is to balance the strengths of the AI tool with the strengths of the human team members. By focusing on collaboration, respect, continuous learning, and a human-centered approach, the integration of the AI tool into the project can be more humanlike and effective.

HYBRID COLLABORATION/INTEGRATION PROMPT

Let's explore another common prompt I use in hybrid environments. This builds on the first prompt. After inputting the personnel information into the first prompt,

HYBRID PROJECT MANAGEMENT PROMPT

//The project involves a hybrid team of developers to code, using agile and a predictive team from the business to drive implementation across the business units. How should the team integrate ideas and synergize? We have four developers, three testers, one architect, a product owner, a scrum master, a sponsor on the side of the business, a program manager, a project manager, and several end users who are stakeholders.//

you can then follow up with this second prompt.

HYBRID PROJECT MANAGEMENT PROMPT 2

//Create a responsibility assignment matrix to spur ideas within the team for integration.//

This prompt yielded the following minimal results :

Roles	Developers	Testers	Architect	Product Owner	Scrum Master	Sponsor	Program Manager	Project Manager	End Users
Integration Ideas	- Pair programming for knowledge sharing	- Collaborative bug triaging	- Conduct architecture review sessions	- Regular feedback sessions with stakeholders	- Facilitate cross-functional collaboration	- Advocate for project goals and resources	- Facilitate cross-team coordination	- Monitor project progress and dependencies	- Gather user feedback through demos and testing

I then followed up with a third prompt.

HYBRID PROJECT MANAGEMENT PROMPT 3

//Create an expanded matrix for all these roles and responsibilities.//

This yielded the following expanded results:

Roles	Developers	Testers	Architect	Product Owner	Scrum Master	Sponsor	Program Manager	Project Manager	End Users
Integration Ideas	- Collaborate on feature development and coding	- Develop and execute test plans	- Define and communicate architectural guidelines and principles	- Prioritize and clarify product requirements	- Facilitate team's adoption of agile practices	- Provide resources and support for the project	- Align project with organizational goals	- Oversee project execution and progress	- Provide feedback on usability and requirements
	- Share knowledge and mentor junior team members	- Perform functional, regression, and UX testing	- Ensure architectural integrity and scalability of the system	- Collaborate with stakeholders to understand user needs and gather feedback	- Remove impediments and foster a productive team environment	- Champion the project within the organization	- Manage program-level risks, dependencies, and communications	- Monitor project timeline, budget, and scope	- Participate in user acceptance testing and provide feedback
	- Collaborate with testers to address defects	- Conduct performance and security testing	- Collaborate with developers to validate technical decisions and ensure adherence to standards	- Collaborate with development team to refine and prioritize the product backlog	- Facilitate meetings and ceremonies such as sprint planning, daily stand-ups, and retrospectives	- Provide strategic guidance and align business objectives with the project	- Monitor and control program-level resources, budgets, and timelines	- Coordinate project activities, resources, and stakeholders	- Participate in requirement elicitation and validation processes
	- Continuously improve code quality and efficiency	- Automate testing and implement test frameworks	- Collaborate with program manager to align architectural strategies with business goals	- Review and provide feedback on user stories and acceptance criteria	- Support the team in self-organization and cross-functional collaboration	- Advocate for necessary changes and resources	- Coordinate dependencies and communication among multiple projects	- Communicate project updates and risks to stakeholders	- Provide input on user experience and suggest improvements
	- Collaborate with architect on system design	- Report and track defects and issues	- Review and provide feedback on technical design decisions	- Ensure backlog is well-groomed and ready for development	- Monitor and report project progress and metrics		- Ensure effective communication and coordination among project teams	- Track project risks and issues and implement mitigation plans	

For a more detailed view of this table, kindly refer to the enlarged version provided on the following page.

Roles	Developers	Testers	Architect	Product Owner	Scrum Master	Sponsor	Program Manager	Project Manager	End Users
	- Collaborate on feature development and coding	- Develop and execute test plans	- Define and communicate architectural guidelines and principles	- Prioritize and clarify product requirements	- Facilitate team's adoption of agile practices	- Provide resources and support for the project	- Align project with organizational goals	- Oversee project execution and progress	- Provide feedback on usability and requirements
	- Share knowledge and mentor junior team members	- Perform functional, regression, and UX testing	- Ensure architectural integrity and scalability of the system	- Collaborate with stakeholders to understand user needs and gather feedback	- Remove impediments and foster a productive team environment	- Champion the project within the organization	- Manage program-level risks, dependencies, and communications	- Monitor project timeline, budget, and scope	- Participate in user acceptance testing and provide feedback
Integration Ideas	- Collaborate with testers to address defects	- Conduct performance and security testing	- Collaborate with developers to validate technical decisions and ensure adherence to standards	- Collaborate with development team to refine and prioritize the product backlog	- Facilitate meetings and ceremonies such as sprint planning, daily stand-ups, and retrospectives	- Provide strategic guidance and align business objectives with the project	- Monitor and control program-level resources, budgets, and timelines	- Coordinate project activities, resources, and stakeholders	- Participate in requirement elicitation and validation processes
	- Continuously improve code quality and efficiency	- Automate testing and implement test frameworks	- Collaborate with program manager to align architectural strategies with business goals	- Review and provide feedback on user stories and acceptance criteria	- Support the team in self-organization and cross-functional collaboration	- Advocate for necessary changes and resources	- Coordinate dependencies and communication among multiple projects	- Communicate project updates and risks to stakeholders	- Provide input on user experience and suggest improvements
	- Collaborate with architect on system design	- Report and track defects and issues	- Review and provide feedback on technical design decisions	- Ensure backlog is well-groomed and ready for development	- Monitor and report project progress and metrics		- Ensure effective communication and coordination among project teams	- Track project risks and issues and implement mitigation plans	

Figure 5: Hybrid Responsibility Assignment Matrix from ChatGPT

113

"And finally," Phill concluded, his watch catching the light as he clicked to the final slide, "let's put theory into practice. Your exercise for today is to implement AI in various hybrid project management scenarios. Remember, this is where the rubber meets the road, so let your creativity and learning shine."

8.4 Exercise: Implementing AI in Hybrid Project Management Scenarios

1. To reinforce the concepts discussed in this chapter, let's engage in an exercise on implementing AI in hybrid project management scenarios. In this exercise, we will explore three different project scenarios that require a hybrid approach, and your task is to identify the most suitable AI tools and techniques to enhance project management outcomes.

Scenario 1: Software Development Project Description: A software development project is underway to create a new application for a client. The project involves a hybrid team of developers working in an agile manner, collaborating with a predictive team from the business side responsible for driving implementation across different business units.

Scenario 2: Infrastructure Upgrade Project Description: An organization is planning a major infrastructure upgrade to enhance its IT capabilities. The project involves a hybrid team consisting of infrastructure specialists and business stakeholders. The team needs to ensure seamless integration of new infrastructure components while minimizing disruptions to ongoing operations.

Scenario 3: Product Launch Project Description: A company is preparing for the launch of a new product in the market. The project involves a hybrid team consisting of marketing, development, and operations professionals. The team needs to effectively manage the product development lifecycle while considering market trends, customer feedback, and regulatory requirements.

2. In each scenario, analyze the project characteristics, stakeholder requirements, and organizational constraints. Consider how AI can be effectively integrated into the project management process to enhance outcomes. Identify the potential benefits and challenges associated with implementing AI and propose strategies to overcome those challenges.

Answer Clues

For example, in the software development project scenario, AI tools like code analysis and automated testing can improve code quality and enhance the efficiency of testing efforts. Natural Language Processing (NLP) techniques can be used to analyze customer feedback and sentiment to inform product decisions. AI-powered project management platforms can facilitate collaboration and provide real-time progress tracking.

Engaging in this exercise will provide practical insights into the application of AI in hybrid project management. By considering the unique requirements of each scenario and identifying suitable AI tools and techniques, you will develop a deeper understanding of how AI can be leveraged to improve project outcomes, drive adaptability, and enhance efficiency.

With the projector humming softly in the background, Phill sat back and observed his class, satisfaction dancing in his eyes. The jesters were now fully engrossed, and the scholars were buzzing with questions. The Project Pathfinder System had once again worked its magic, guiding them on their journey through the complex maze of project management.

CHAPTER NINE: AI IN SCRUM PRACTICES

> ❝
> *"Refusing to consider AI, is refusing to be truly Agile! Like the Blockbusters of this world, one could be left behind!"*

With a swift rotation of his wrist, Phill checked the time on one of his many exquisite watches. Satisfied that he was still on track, he confidently ushered in the next chapter of their learning journey. "Alright, class," he began, his vibrant tie swinging as he paced the room, "it's time to journey into Scrum and AI."

First things first," Phill asserted, flipping to a new slide deck on the screen. "Let's refresh our memories about the Scrum framework. Remember, Scrum is not a methodology, but a framework to embrace complexity and adaptability in product development and project management." The room, filled with a mix of serious scholars and mischievous jesters, listened intently as he illuminated the essence of Scrum.

"Scrum is an iterative and incremental framework for software development. It is based on the idea of breaking down a large project into smaller, more manageable tasks. These tasks are then completed in short sprints, typically lasting two weeks." He began.

> **9.1 Introduction to Scrum Framework**
>
> In this chapter, we explore the integration of artificial intelligence (AI) technologies within the Scrum framework, a popular agile project management methodology. Scrum emphasizes iterative development, collaboration, and adaptability, making it well-suited for dynamic and complex projects. By leveraging AI, organizations can further enhance Scrum practices and improve team performance and project outcomes.
>
> - We begin by providing an introduction to the Scrum framework. We explain the key principles of Scrum, such as the roles of the Scrum Master, Product Owner, and Development Team, as well as the core Scrum artifacts and ceremonies.
> - Understanding the fundamental concepts of Scrum is essential to appreciate how AI can be integrated into its practices.

Scrum is a lightweight and flexible framework. It is designed to be easy to understand and implement, making it accessible to teams and organizations. With its adaptability, Scrum can be tailored to suit various project types and teams of different sizes. By following the Scrum framework, teams can effectively manage their work in an iterative and collaborative manner, enabling them to deliver value in a transparent and efficient way. Scrum has a 3-5-3 configuration.

The 3-5-3 of Scrum refers to the three key roles, five events, and three artifacts that constitute the Scrum framework.

1. Roles:
    - Product Owner: Represents the stakeholders and defines the project vision, prioritizes the product backlog, and ensures the team delivers maximum value.

- Scrum Master: Facilitates the Scrum process, removes impediments, and ensures the team adheres to Scrum principles and practices.

- Development Team: Self-organizing and cross-functional, responsible for delivering the product increments during each sprint.

2. Events:

- Sprint: A timeboxed iteration (usually 2-4 weeks) in which the team completes a set of product backlog items and delivers a potentially releasable increment.

- Sprint Planning: The team collaboratively plans the work to be done during the upcoming sprint.

- Daily Scrum: A daily 15-minute stand-up meeting where team members synchronize their work, discuss progress, and identify any impediments.

- Sprint Review: Held at the end of the sprint, the team presents the completed work to stakeholders and obtains feedback for future iterations.

- Sprint Retrospective: Occurring after the Sprint Review, the team reflects on their collaboration, processes, and identifies improvements for the next sprint.

3. Artifacts:

- Product Backlog: A prioritized list of features, user stories, and tasks that represent the product requirements.

- Sprint Backlog: The subset of items from the product backlog that the team commits to completing during a sprint.

- Increment: The sum of all completed product backlog items at the end of a sprint, representing a potentially releasable version of the product.

The 3-5-3 of Scrum provides a concise overview of the key elements in the framework, enabling teams to understand and effectively implement Scrum principles in their projects.

Phill steered the conversation towards the role of AI in Scrum. "With AI," he elucidated, "planning and estimation in Scrum can become significantly more efficient." He explained the ways AI tools could provide more accurate effort estimations and streamline the planning process.

AI can be used to improve the planning and estimation of Scrum projects. AI can be used to analyze historical data, identify trends, and make predictions. This information can be used to help Scrum teams better estimate the effort required to complete tasks and to plan sprints.

For example, AI can be used to analyze historical sprint data to identify patterns in the amount of work that is completed in each sprint. This information can then be used to make more accurate estimates for future sprints.

AI can also be used to predict the likelihood of success for different project scenarios. This information can be used to help Scrum teams make informed decisions about how to allocate resources and manage risks.

9.2 AI Applications in Scrum Planning and Estimation

Planning and estimation are critical aspects of Scrum, as they set the foundation for successful project execution. AI technologies can assist in automating and streamlining these processes, leading to more accurate and efficient planning and estimation outcomes.

- AI algorithms can analyze historical project data, user stories, and other relevant information to provide insights and recommendations for better planning and estimation.
- AI tools can identify patterns, predict resource requirements, and help determine the most optimal backlog prioritization.
- By leveraging AI in planning and estimation, Scrum teams can enhance their decision-making capabilities and improve the accuracy of their project forecasts.

AI can be used to track the performance of Scrum teams. AI can be used to collect data on team activity, such as the number of tasks completed, the time spent on tasks, and the number of defects found. This data can then be used to identify trends and patterns in team performance.

For example, AI can be used to track the amount of time that is spent on each task in a sprint. This information can then be used to identify tasks that are taking longer than expected. This information can then be used to improve the team's process for completing these tasks.

AI can also be used to predict the likelihood of success for different team scenarios. This information can be used to help Scrum teams make informed decisions about how to improve their performance.

When it comes to AI, data tables like the one below can be further analyzed to glean patterns, identify trends, and make accurate predictions. The quality of the input data significantly impacts the quality of the information generated by AI algorithms. Therefore, ensuring good data input is crucial to obtain reliable and valuable insights.

In this dummy data, we have five software modules (Module A, Module B, Module C, Module D, and Module E) with lines of code written for each module in each month from January to December.

Module	January	February	March	April	May	June	July	August	September	October	November	December
Module A	250	200	150	180	300	280	220	250	200	150	180	300
Module B	180	150	200	220	240	280	300	250	180	150	200	220
Module C	220	250	180	200	150	180	200	220	250	180	200	150
Module D	200	220	240	280	300	250	180	150	200	220	240	280
Module E	150	180	200	150	200	220	240	280	300	250	180	150

Figure 6: Sample Team Data of Lines of Code Written Per Module

By feeding the data table into AI models and algorithms, we can leverage machine learning techniques to identify hidden patterns and relationships within the dataset. These patterns can provide valuable insights into the team's productivity, module-wise code development trends, and overall project progress.

Through data analysis, AI can identify correlations between different variables, such as the impact of team size, module complexity, or external factors like deadlines or resource availability, on the lines of code written. This analysis can help project managers and stakeholders gain a deeper understanding of the project's dynamics and make informed decisions.

Additionally, AI algorithms can utilize historical data to make predictions about future code development. By recognizing patterns and extrapolating from past performance, AI can provide valuable forecasts regarding lines of code development for upcoming months or even predict potential bottlenecks or deviations from expected progress.

However, it is important to note that while AI can provide insightful predictions, it should be used in conjunction with human judgment and expertise. AI algorithms are only as good as the data they are trained on, and human domain knowledge is crucial for interpreting and contextualizing the generated information. Human oversight and critical thinking are necessary to validate the predictions and make informed decisions based on the AI-generated insights.

As Phill dove deeper into the interplay of AI and Scrum, Phill explored how AI could enhance team performance tracking. "Imagine having a virtual assistant that could measure performance in real-time, identify bottlenecks, and even suggest improvements!" he exclaimed, highlighting the potential benefits of AI in Scrum team management.

9.3 AI-Enhanced Scrum Team Performance Tracking

In this section, we move into how AI can enhance Scrum team performance tracking. Monitoring team performance is crucial for identifying bottlenecks, improving productivity, and ensuring project success.

- AI technologies can provide real-time insights and analytics to track team performance metrics, identify areas for improvement, and facilitate data-driven decision making.
- We explore how AI can assist in tracking key performance indicators (KPIs), such as sprint velocity, burn-down charts, and team collaboration metrics.
- AI algorithms can analyze team interactions, identify communication patterns, and provide actionable recommendations to enhance collaboration and productivity.
- Additionally, AI-powered dashboards and visualizations can provide stakeholders with clear and comprehensive performance reports.

Let's revisit our data table and see how AI could be leveraged in its analysis.

Module	January	February	March	April	May	June	July	August	September	October	November	December
Module A	250	200	150	180	300	280	220	250	200	150	180	300
Module B	180	150	200	220	240	280	300	250	180	150	200	220
Module C	220	250	180	200	150	180	200	220	250	180	200	150
Module D	200	220	240	280	300	250	180	150	200	220	240	280
Module E	150	180	200	150	200	220	240	280	300	250	180	150

AI Data Analysis Ideas

From a Scrum and Agile perspective, you could interpret and analyze this data in several ways to optimize your team's productivity and manage your software development process more effectively:

1. **Velocity Analysis**: The number of lines of code can be used as a proxy for estimating how much work the team can accomplish during each sprint. Calculate the average number of lines of code produced per month for each module to determine your team's velocity. This can help in future planning.

2. **Workload Distribution**: Determine if the workload is evenly distributed among the modules. If one module consistently requires more coding work, you may need to allocate more resources to it or consider refactoring it for efficiency.

3. **Trend Analysis**: Look for trends in coding productivity for each module over time. If productivity is increasing, it may suggest the team is becoming more familiar with the module or that recent changes have led to efficiency improvements. If productivity is decreasing, it may be a sign of technical debt, a need for training, or other blockers.

4. **Bottleneck Identification**: If you see that coding progress fluctuates significantly from month to month for a specific module, it could indicate potential bottlenecks or issues in the development process. Identifying these can help you address the underlying problems.

5. **Efficiency Improvements**: If the lines of code for a module are significantly decreasing over time without a corresponding decrease in functionality, this might be an indication of efficiency improvements or effective refactoring.

6. **Sprint Planning**: Use this data to inform future sprint planning. By understanding the trends in lines of code for each module, you can more accurately predict how much work can be done in future sprints.

7. **Backlog Management**: If you see a module consistently requiring more lines of code than others, it might indicate that more user stories or tasks are being added to the backlog for that module. This could impact the priority of tasks in your product backlog.

8. **Technical Debt Assessment**: If a module has a steadily increasing amount of code over time without a corresponding increase in functionality or features, it could suggest accruing technical debt that might slow down future development.

Remember, while lines of code can be a helpful metric in some cases, it does not necessarily reflect the quality of the code, the complexity of the tasks, or the value delivered to the end user. Other factors and metrics should be considered as well when managing a project in an Agile or Scrum environment.

General AI Data Analysis

There are several types of analyses you could perform using this or similar data. Here are a few examples:

1. **Descriptive Analysis**: This could involve calculating the mean, median, mode, and standard deviation for each module to provide insights into the central tendency and dispersion of usage.

2. **Trend Analysis**: Identify if there's a pattern in the usage of each module over time. You could plot the monthly usage over time to visually inspect any trends, seasonality, or cyclical patterns.

3. **Comparative Analysis**: Compare the usage of different modules for each month. This could identify which module is used the most or least during specific months, and might reveal some underlying patterns or trends.

4. **Peak and Off-peak Usage Analysis**: Identify the months with the highest (peak) and lowest (off-peak) usage for each module.

5. **Growth Analysis**: Calculate the month-on-month and year-on-year growth rates in usage for each module.

6. **Correlation Analysis**: Examine if the usage of different modules is correlated. For example, when usage of Module A increases, does usage of Module B also increase?

7. **Cluster Analysis**: Group the months based on the usage of different modules. This could potentially identify any clusters of months with similar usage patterns.

8. **Outlier Detection**: Identify any months that had unusually high or low usage compared to the general trend.

9. **Forecasting**: Based on past trends, forecast future usage for each module. This can be done using various techniques like moving averages, exponential smoothing, or even more complex models like ARIMA if the data exhibits a pattern or trend.

These analyses could provide valuable insights into the usage patterns of these modules and aid in decision-making, planning, and strategy development for future use or enhancements.

Finally, Phill unveiled the day's exercise: "Here's your chance to explore how AI can transform Scrum practices. Consider how an AI tool can aid in Scrum planning, estimation, and team performance tracking. Don't just think theoretically; be creative and practical."

With that, he sat back, looking across the sea of thoughtful faces. His mix of jesters and scholars had matured into a cohort of future project managers, each one eager to explore the frontier of AI in Scrum practices. The room hummed with a new energy, as the class dove headfirst into the intriguing world of AI-enhanced Scrum.

Conclusion

AI can be used to improve the effectiveness of Scrum practices. By using AI to analyze data, identify trends, and make predictions, Scrum teams can make better decisions about planning, estimation, and performance tracking.

9.4 Exercise: Leveraging AI for Scrum Practices

Case Study: Team AgileBoost - Improving Scrum Practices with AI

Team AgileBoost is a software development team working on a complex project for a large client. They've been using Scrum practices for several years. Recently, they've been struggling with two major issues: effort estimation and maintaining a well-prioritized product backlog.

The team has noticed that their estimates for user stories often do not accurately reflect the actual effort required. This inaccurate estimation has led to several sprints not completing as planned, leading to delays in the project timeline.

In addition, AgileBoost's product backlog has become cluttered and unwieldy. As a result, important tasks sometimes get overlooked, and the team members are not always working on the most valuable features.

To address these issues, AgileBoost has decided to leverage AI tools. They are using an AI-powered project management tool that assists with both effort estimation and backlog prioritization.

For effort estimation, the tool uses historical project data and machine learning algorithms to predict how much effort each user story will require. It takes into account factors such as the complexity of the story, the team's velocity, and the individual team members' capabilities.

For backlog prioritization, the tool uses an algorithm that considers several factors, such as the business value of each feature, its dependencies, and its complexity. It helps the Product Owner keep the backlog well-organized and ensures the team is always working on the most valuable features.

Discussion Questions:

1. How is AI helping Team AgileBoost improve their Scrum practices and enhance their output?
2. What potential challenges might Team AgileBoost face when integrating AI into their Scrum practices?
3. How should Team AgileBoost measure the success or effectiveness of their AI integration?
4. Are there any other areas of Team AgileBoost's Scrum practices where AI could be beneficial?
5. What ethical considerations should Team AgileBoost bear in mind when using AI tools in their Scrum practices?

CHAPTER TEN: AI IN KANBAN PRACTICES

"Kanban, teams can unleash the potential of AI to optimize their workflow and drive efficiency to new heights!"

A chorus of hushed whispers and soft laughter filled the room as Phill adjusted his brightly patterned tie, the myriad colors a stark contrast to his professional suit. He cleared his throat and silence immediately descended on the classroom, jesters and scholars alike waiting in eager anticipation.

"Okay, explorers and adventurers," Phill began, striking a perfect balance between seriousness and jest, "Let's embark on our next journey - Kanban practices in the realm of Artificial Intelligence."

"First, we revisit the Kanban approach," Phill instructed, setting the stage with a vivid explanation of Kanban basics. "Remember, Kanban is more than a framework; it is a lens through which we visualize and manage our workflow." He went into the details, bridging the gap between abstract concepts and tangible applications.

10.1 Introduction to Kanban

In this chapter, we explore the integration of artificial intelligence (AI) technologies within the Kanban methodology. Kanban is an agile project management approach that focuses on visualizing work, limiting work in progress (WIP), and optimizing workflow efficiency.

By incorporating AI, organizations can further enhance Kanban practices and improve productivity, predictability, and overall project success.

- We provide an introduction to the Kanban methodology, explaining its core principles, such as visualizing work, setting WIP limits, and continuously improving the workflow.
- Understanding the fundamental concepts of Kanban is essential to appreciate how AI can be integrated into its practices.

Kanban is a process management framework that aims to improve the flow and efficiency of work within a team or organization. It is based on the principles of visualizing work, limiting work-in-progress (WIP), and managing flow.

At its core, Kanban provides a visual representation of work through a Kanban board. The board consists of columns representing different stages of the workflow, and tasks or work items are represented as cards or sticky notes that move through the columns as they progress. This visual representation allows team members to have a clear and shared understanding of the work in progress and facilitates transparency and collaboration.

One of the key principles of Kanban is limiting the amount of work that can be in progress at any given time. This helps prevent overloading the team and promotes focus and timely completion of work. By setting explicit WIP limits for each column on the Kanban board, teams can identify bottlenecks and ensure a smooth and balanced flow of work throughout the workflow.

Kanban also emphasizes the importance of managing flow. This involves actively monitoring and optimizing the movement of work items through the workflow, ensuring that there are no delays or blockers. By continuously assessing and improving flow, teams can identify and address inefficiencies, reduce lead times, and increase overall productivity.

Another characteristic of Kanban is its lightweight and flexible nature. It is designed to be easy to understand and implement, making it accessible to teams of various sizes and industries. Kanban can be adapted to fit the specific needs and context of different projects and teams, allowing for customization and continuous improvement.

In Kanban, there are no predefined roles or ceremonies like in some other project management methodologies. Instead, it encourages self-organization and empowerment of team members to collaborate and make decisions. It promotes a culture of continuous improvement and encourages teams to regularly reflect on their processes and adapt them for better outcomes.

Overall, Kanban provides a simple yet powerful framework for managing work, improving efficiency, and promoting collaboration within teams. Its emphasis on visualization, WIP limits, and flow management enables teams to optimize their processes, deliver value more consistently, and adapt to changing project requirements.

Once they were rooted in the foundations of Kanban, Phill ventured into the uncharted territories of AI integration. "How can we enhance our Kanban boards with AI?" he posed, opening the floor to speculation before guiding the class through various applications of AI, from predictive analytics to real-time updates and automated task allocation.

10.2 AI-Driven Kanban Board Optimization

Next, we explore how AI can drive Kanban board optimization. The Kanban board is a visual representation of the workflow, typically consisting of columns representing different stages of work and cards representing individual tasks. AI technologies can analyze historical data, user behavior, and other relevant information to optimize the layout and configuration of the Kanban board.

AI algorithms can suggest improvements to the board's structure, such as column reordering, resizing WIP limits, and dynamically adjusting workflow policies. AI can also provide insights into task prioritization, identifying bottlenecks, and facilitating the smooth flow of work. By leveraging AI in Kanban board optimization, organizations can streamline their processes, reduce waste, and improve overall efficiency.

AI can be used to optimize Kanban boards. AI can be used to analyze historical data, identify trends, and make predictions. This information can be used to help Kanban teams optimize their boards for efficiency and effectiveness.

For example, AI can be used to analyze historical Kanban board data to identify patterns in the amount of work that is completed in each column. This information can then be used to make more informed decisions about how to optimize the board. AI can also be used to predict the likelihood of success for different board scenarios. This information can be used to help Kanban teams make informed decisions about how to improve their boards.

AI algorithms can play a valuable role in suggesting improvements to the structure of a Kanban board, optimizing its configuration, and facilitating the smooth flow of work. By analyzing historical data, real-time information, and patterns within the workflow, AI algorithms can provide actionable insights and recommendations for enhancing the board's effectiveness.

Column Reordering: AI algorithms can analyze data related to task completion times, dependencies, and interrelationships to identify patterns and suggest optimal column ordering. By reordering the columns based on the flow and dependencies of work, teams can minimize handoffs and reduce wait times, leading to a more efficient workflow.

Resizing WIP Limits: AI algorithms can analyze historical data, team capacity, and cycle times to provide recommendations for resizing Work-in-Progress (WIP) limits. By dynamically adjusting WIP limits, teams can balance their workload, prevent bottlenecks, and maintain a steady flow of work.

Dynamic Workflow Policies: AI algorithms can evaluate the current state of the workflow and recommend adjustments to workflow policies based on real-time data. For example, if a particular column consistently becomes a bottleneck, the AI algorithm can suggest modifying the policies, such as adding additional resources or reallocating tasks, to optimize the flow of work.

Task Prioritization: AI algorithms can analyze various factors, such as task dependencies, urgency, and business value, to provide insights into task prioritization. By considering multiple variables, AI algorithms can suggest the optimal sequence of tasks to maximize productivity and meet project objectives.

Identifying Bottlenecks: AI algorithms can monitor the flow of work through the Kanban board, detect patterns, and identify potential bottlenecks or areas of congestion. By highlighting these bottlenecks, teams can proactively address them, redistribute work, and optimize the flow to ensure smooth progress.

Facilitating Flow of Work: By analyzing the data and patterns within the Kanban workflow, AI algorithms can provide insights into how work items can move smoothly through the process. This may involve suggesting adjustments to WIP limits, reordering tasks, or proposing process improvements to reduce friction and enable a more seamless flow.

"AI isn't just about optimizing task assignments," Phill continued, moving into the subtleties of flow and cycle time analysis. He illustrated how AI can assist in monitoring workflows, identifying potential bottlenecks, and providing recommendations to improve process efficiency and delivery times.

10.3 AI-Enabled Flow and Cycle Time Analysis

In this section, we hone in on how AI can enable flow and cycle time analysis in Kanban practices. Flow and cycle time analysis involves measuring and analyzing the time it takes for work items to move through the workflow. By understanding and optimizing flow and cycle time, organizations can improve predictability, identify process inefficiencies, and make data-driven decisions.

We explore how AI technologies can analyze historical data, monitor real-time work progress, and provide insights into flow and cycle time patterns. AI algorithms can identify trends, detect anomalies, and suggest strategies for reducing cycle time and improving overall flow.

By leveraging AI-enabled flow and cycle time analysis, organizations can enhance their ability to deliver work items on time, optimize resource utilization, and identify areas for continuous improvement.

"So, you know how we're always looking for ways to get better at what we do, right? Well, that's where AI comes into play, especially when we talk about flow and cycle time analysis in Kanban practices. It's all about making the most of what AI can do—like analyzing data, recognizing patterns, and monitoring things in real-time." Phill paused for a gulp of mineral water.

"In a nutshell, flow and cycle time analysis is about figuring out how long it takes for tasks to make it through the workflow. It's like a backstage pass to see how efficient our processes really are, and it lets us make tweaks based on actual data.

Now, AI is like this detective who's really good at spotting patterns. It can look at data from past Kanban cycles—things like cycle times, how much we're getting done, and task details. From there, it can work out where we're seeing the same things happen over and over again, or where things might be getting stuck. This kind of understanding can help us get a grip on how our processes work, find what needs fixing, and fine-tune our workflow.

But that's not all! AI can also keep an eye on things as they happen. By working alongside our Kanban tools, it can track tasks, gather up-to-the-minute data, and keep us in the loop about how work is flowing and how long it's taking. It's like having a live feed into our workflow, spotting anything out of the ordinary that might be slowing us down." At this point Kevin was seen struggling with sleep, fighting to keep his eyes open. Phill strolled over towards Kevin's desk and continued, rather loud.

"What's really cool is that by looking at past data and keeping tabs on things in real-time, AI can help us get a handle on how flow and cycle time change. It can point out trends, blips, and any logjams, and even suggest how we could cut down on cycle time and streamline how work gets done. This way, we can make decisions that are rooted in data, tweak our processes, and work towards a workflow that's more predictable and efficient."

"So yes, AI tech really can boost flow and cycle time analysis in Kanban practices. It can look at past data, keep an eye on what's happening now, and give us the lowdown on how flow and cycle time are changing. It's like having a secret weapon that helps us see what's really going on, spot where we can get better, and make calls that will actually enhance our Kanban workflow."

"As always," Phill concluded, "we end with an exercise. Today, I challenge you to explore ways AI could be integrated into Kanban practices. Don't forget to consider all aspects, from board optimization to flow and cycle time analysis." Kevin had fully revived from his slumber was scribbling frantically to recover from his mid-day daze.

With the sound of the projector humming in the background, Phill leaned back and surveyed his class, a mix of deep contemplation and simmering excitement etched across their faces. Another successful class in the making, another step forward in understanding how AI could revolutionize project management methodologies.

10.4 Exercise: "Exploring the Intersection of AI and Kanban: A Multifaceted Approach"

Objective: This exercise is designed to encourage deep understanding of the integration of Artificial Intelligence (AI) into Kanban systems, identify potential benefits, and discuss ethical considerations.

Materials needed: Access to internet resources, research papers on AI and Kanban, and preferably an AI Kanban software demo.

Steps:

1. Integration of AI in Kanban: Start by researching different ways AI algorithms can be integrated into Kanban practices to optimize workflow and improve efficiency. Outline specific AI techniques and algorithms that can be utilized, and provide examples of companies that have successfully implemented these measures.

2. Benefits of AI in Kanban: Identify and discuss the potential benefits of using AI in Kanban. Examine how AI might enhance decision-making and performance tracking in a Kanban system. Discuss whether these benefits would be universally applicable or dependent on certain factors like company size, industry type, or the complexity of the workflow.

3. Ethical Considerations in AI and Kanban: Consider the ethical aspects when integrating AI into Kanban. Explore issues of AI bias, privacy concerns, and job displacement. Propose solutions or strategies to address these concerns. For instance, how can AI bias be minimized? What measures can be put in place to protect privacy? How can companies manage potential job displacement due to AI?

4. In-depth Case Study Analysis: Choose a real or hypothetical company that uses or plans to use AI in their Kanban system. Apply your findings from the previous steps to this case study. Discuss how AI could be integrated, the potential benefits, and how ethical considerations could be handled in this particular case.

5. Reflection: Write a reflection on your findings and the case study analysis. Discuss the implications of AI integration in Kanban and whether you believe it to be generally beneficial, or if its effectiveness is situation-dependent.

6. Future Outlook: Speculate on the future of AI in Kanban, taking into consideration technological advancements, ethical implications, and business needs.

CHAPTER ELEVEN: DATA ANALYTICS AND AI IN PROJECT MANAGEMENT

> "
>
> *"In the realm of AI, data is not just the new oil, it's the refinery, the gas station, and the car. It is through careful and rigorous analysis of this data that AI truly learns to drive innovation forward."*

"Alright, jesters and scholars," Phill declared, striding across the room with an infectious enthusiasm that managed to draw even the most wayward jesters' attention. His eye-catching tie danced with his movements, and his polished watch gleamed under the fluorescent lights. "We're going to tackle a new frontier today: Data Analytics and AI in Project Management."

"Let's start with understanding why Data Analytics is so important in project management," Phill kicked off the day's lesson. His voice echoed in the room as he underlined the role of data in driving decision-making, predicting trends, and gauging project health.

> **11.1 Importance of Data Analytics in Project Management**
> In this chapter, we explore the significance of data analytics in project management and how it can be augmented by artificial intelligence (AI) technologies. Data analytics plays a crucial role in project management by enabling organizations to extract valuable insights from project-related data. By harnessing the power of AI, project managers can enhance their decision-making processes, improve project performance, and drive successful outcomes.
>
> We discuss the importance of data analytics in project management, including its ability to identify trends, patterns, and correlations within project data. Data analytics provides project managers with a comprehensive understanding of project performance, risks, and opportunities. We emphasize the value of collecting and analyzing relevant project data throughout the project lifecycle to enable data-driven decision making.

Data analytics is the process of collecting, cleaning, analyzing, and interpreting data to gain insights that can be used to improve decision-making. In project management, data analytics can be used to improve the following:

- Project planning: Data analytics can be used to analyze historical data to identify trends and patterns that can be used to improve project planning. For example, data analytics can be used to identify tasks that are typically completed late or over budget. This information can then be used to adjust the project plan to account for these risks.

- Project execution: Data analytics can be used to track project progress and identify potential problems. For example, data analytics can be used to track the amount of time that tasks are taking to complete. This information can then be used to identify tasks that are at risk of being late or over budget.

- Project risk management: Data analytics can be used to identify and assess project risks. For example, data analytics can be used to track historical data on project risks. This information can then be used to identify risks that are more likely to occur.

- Project performance reporting: Data analytics can be used to create reports that track project performance. These reports can be used to identify areas where the project is performing well and areas where improvement is needed.

Moving on, Phill started discussing the potential of AI in project risk analysis. "With AI, we can assess risks not just based on our experience and intuition, but also backed by solid data," he stated. Through various real-life examples, he showcased how AI algorithms could help detect patterns, anticipate risks, and prescribe mitigation strategies.

11.2 AI-Powered Project Risk Analysis

Risk management is an essential aspect of project management, and AI technologies can significantly enhance the identification, assessment, and mitigation of project risks. AI algorithms can process large volumes of data, including historical project data, industry benchmarks, and external factors, to provide comprehensive risk analysis.

We explore how AI can automate the identification of potential risks, analyze their impact and likelihood, and provide recommendations for risk mitigation strategies. AI-powered risk analysis can help project managers proactively manage risks, allocate resources efficiently, and ensure project success. We discuss the benefits and considerations of using AI in project risk analysis, emphasizing the importance of human expertise in interpreting and implementing the insights generated by AI.

AI can be used to power project risk analysis. AI can be used to analyze historical data, identify trends, and make predictions about future risks. This information can be used to help project managers identify and assess project risks.

For example, AI can be used to analyze historical data on project risks. This information can then be used to identify risks that are more likely to occur. AI can also be used to predict the likelihood of different risks occurring. This information can be used to help project managers prioritize risks and allocate resources accordingly. Let's take a look at how AI has been useful in general risk management:

1. **Healthcare:** AI has been instrumental in analyzing medical data to identify disease patterns and predict health risks. For example, Google's DeepMind developed an AI that can analyze eye

scans to detect signs of age-related macular degeneration and diabetic retinopathy, potentially preventing vision loss in patients.

2. **Finance:** Banks and other financial institutions use AI to analyze transaction data and detect suspicious activities that might indicate fraud or money laundering. This helps them mitigate financial risk and protect their customers. For instance, MasterCard uses AI-based decision intelligence technology to detect and prevent fraudulent transactions in real-time.

3. **Cybersecurity:** AI systems can analyze vast amounts of data traffic to detect anomalies that suggest potential cyber threats. These systems can identify patterns indicative of malware, phishing attempts, and other forms of cyber-attacks, providing warnings and averting possible data breaches. Companies like Darktrace employ AI for advanced threat detection and response.

4. **Climate Science:** AI is being used to analyze climate data to predict natural disasters such as hurricanes, floods, or forest fires. By analyzing weather patterns, atmospheric data, and geological information, these AI models can predict potential disasters and help authorities take preventive measures. For example, IBM's AI-based weather forecasting system can provide high-resolution, global weather prediction to improve preparedness for severe weather conditions.

5. **Manufacturing:** AI is used in predictive maintenance to analyze data from machinery and predict potential mechanical failures before they occur. This can prevent expensive downtime in manufacturing and other industries. Companies like Siemens use AI technologies to predict and prevent equipment malfunctions.

Remember, while these are successful examples of AI and data analysis averting risks, they don't eliminate the need for human oversight. AI tools provide insights and augment human decision-making abilities; they do not replace them.

Diving deeper, Phill turned his attention to how AI could revolutionize performance metrics and reporting. "Imagine a world where AI not only tracks and reports performance but also predicts future performance based on past data," he said, setting the tone for a stimulating discussion on the potential of AI in project performance management.

11.3 AI-Driven Performance Metrics and Reporting

AI can drive performance metrics and reporting in project management. Effective monitoring and reporting of project performance is crucial for project success and stakeholder communication. AI technologies can automate data collection, analysis, and reporting processes, enabling project managers to access real-time performance metrics and generate accurate and timely reports.

AI can analyze project data to generate key performance indicators (KPIs), visualize project progress, and provide insights into areas of improvement. AI-driven performance metrics and reporting enhance project managers' ability to make informed decisions, identify performance gaps, and communicate project status effectively. We also highlight the importance of ensuring data integrity and privacy when leveraging AI for performance metrics and reporting.

AI can also be used to drive performance metrics and reporting in project management. AI can be used to collect data on project performance, analyze the data, and generate reports. These reports can be used to track project performance and identify areas where improvement is needed.

For example, AI can be used to collect data on the amount of time that tasks are taking to complete. This data can then be used to generate reports that track project progress and identify tasks that are at risk of being late or over budget. AI can also be used to generate reports that identify areas where the project is performing well and areas where improvement is needed. Let's examine AI's prowess with Earned Value Management.

Try the following prompt with an AI tool such as ChatGPT. Copy and paste the entire text and table:

EARNED VALUE PROMPT

Prompt

// Analyze the following datasheet from an earned value perspective:

	JAN	FEB	MARCH
PLANNED VALUE	$ 5,000.00	$ 7,500.00	$ 5,354.00
EARNED VALUE	$ 3,500.00	$ 7,450.00	$ 5,234.00
ACTUAL COST	$ 6,000.00	$ 6,900.00	$ 5,800.00

//

OUTPUT

Let's first understand the three key metrics used in earned value analysis:

1. **Planned Value (PV)**: This is the estimated cost for the planned work.

2. **Earned Value (EV)**: This is the value of the actual work completed.

3. **Actual Cost (AC)**: This is the actual cost incurred for the work completed.

Now, let's calculate some useful indicators:

Cost Variance (CV) is calculated as: CV = EV - AC A negative CV indicates the project is over budget.

Schedule Variance (SV) is calculated as: SV = EV - PV A negative SV indicates the project is behind schedule.

Cost Performance Index (CPI) is calculated as: CPI = EV / AC A CPI of less than 1 indicates a cost overrun.

Schedule Performance Index (SPI) is calculated as: SPI = EV / PV An SPI of less than 1 indicates the project is behind schedule.

So, let's calculate these metrics for each month:

January:

CV = $3,500 - $6,000 = -$2,500

SV = $3,500 - $5,000 = -$1,500

CPI = $3,500 / $6,000 = 0.58

SPI = $3,500 / $5,000 = 0.7

February:

CV = $7,450 - $6,900 = $550

SV = $7,450 - $7,500 = -$50

CPI = $7,450 / $6,900 = 1.08

SPI = $7,450 / $7,500 = 0.993

March:

CV = $5,234 - $5,800 = -$566

SV = $5,234 - $5,354 = -$120

CPI = $5,234 / $5,800 = 0.90

SPI = $5,234 / $5,354 = 0.978

One more prompt to glean additional findings!

EARNED VALUE PROMPT			
Prompt **// Comment on the trends observed in this table**			
	JAN	**FEB**	**MARCH**
PLANNED VALUE	$ 5,000.00	$ 7,500.00	$ 5,354.00
EARNED VALUE	$ 3,500.00	$ 7,450.00	$ 5,234.00
ACTUAL COST	$ 6,000.00	$ 6,900.00	$ 5,800.00
//			

OUTPUT

January:
CPI = $3,500 / $6,000 = 0.58
SPI = $3,500 / $5,000 = 0.7

February:
CPI = $7,450 / $6,900 = 1.08
SPI = $7,450 / $7,500 = 0.993

March:
CPI = $5,234 / $5,800 = 0.90
SPI = $5,234 / $5,354 = 0.978

Analysis:
January:
The CPI and SPI are both less than 1, indicating the project is both over budget and behind schedule.

February:
The CPI is greater than 1 and the SPI is slightly less than 1, which means the project has performed under budget but is slightly behind schedule. This indicates an improvement in cost management compared to January but the schedule efficiency still needs improvement.

March:
Both CPI and SPI are less than 1, but they are closer to 1 compared to January. This suggests that although the project is again over budget and slightly behind schedule, it's closer to being on track than it was in January.

Overall, the project seems to be struggling with both cost and schedule efficiency, with the exception of cost efficiency in February. The project management team should focus on improving both cost management and scheduling to get the project back on track.

It's impressive to witness the capability of ChatGPT in performing an insightful analysis of the provided Earned Value table. Despite the table's relatively small size, the AI was able to efficiently extract valuable insights. This suggests that ChatGPT could perform equally well, if not better, with larger data sets. The rapidity and accuracy of such analyses clearly demonstrate the transformative potential of AI in data-driven decision making.

Once more, the class fell silent as students leaned into the task, the occasional scratch of a pen or tap of a keyboard the only sounds breaking the silence. Phill's watch ticked steadily, marking the passage of time as the room buzzed with the energy of a class on the frontier of knowledge, pushing the boundaries of project management with each passing second.

"Time for some practical application!" Phill declared, outlining an exercise that blended the day's lessons. "I want you to explore ways to apply data analytics and AI in project management. Think about risk analysis, performance metrics, reporting, and other areas you find interesting."

Conclusion

Data analytics and AI are powerful tools that can be used to improve project management. By using these tools, project managers can make better decisions, identify and assess risks, and track project performance.

The exercise in this chapter provides an opportunity to practice applying data analytics and AI in project management. By completing this exercise, you will gain a better understanding of how these tools can be used to improve the success of projects.

11.4 Exercise: Data Analytics and AI Application in Project Management

Objective: This exercise is designed to enhance your understanding and application of data analytics and AI in project management. You'll be asked to consider various project scenarios, identify appropriate data analytics techniques, AI tools, and propose strategies for their effective implementation.

Scenario: You are a project manager at an IT firm. Your firm has been managing projects using traditional project management methods. Given the increasing complexity and scale of projects, your firm decides to leverage data analytics and AI to improve project management practices. Your task is to propose how to implement this change.

Instructions:

1. **Data Analytics Integration:**

   - Identify three key areas in your project management process where data analytics could significantly improve outcomes.

   - For each area, describe the kind of data that would be needed, how this data could be collected, and which data analytics techniques could be used to generate insights.

2. **AI Implementation:**

   - Propose two AI tools or systems that could be integrated into the project management process.

   - Explain how these tools could enhance decision-making, risk management, or performance tracking.

3. **Strategy for Implementation:**

   - Considering organizational context and project constraints, outline a strategy for implementing data analytics and AI in your firm's project management practice.

   - Consider potential challenges, including data availability, algorithm selection, employee training, and the ethical implications of AI use.

4. **Case Study:**

   - Choose a past project managed by your firm and imagine that data analytics and AI tools were available at the time.

   - How could these technologies have altered the management and outcome of the project?

Deliverable: Prepare a detailed report outlining your answers and present your findings to the class. Through this exercise, you will gain practical insights into the application of data analytics and AI in project management and a deeper understanding of how these technologies can enhance decision-making and project outcomes.

Remember, the goal is to think critically about the integration of data analytics and AI into project management, taking into consideration the specific needs and constraints of your organization. There isn't a one-size-fits-all answer, and creative, well-reasoned strategies are encouraged.

CHAPTER TWELVE: AI IMPLEMENTATION AND ADOPTION STRATEGIES

> "*Artificial intelligence is not just a technology, it's a transformational catalyst.*"

"Good morning, pioneers and trailblazers," Phill greeted, straightening his brightly patterned tie. His watch collection was the topic of whispers among the jesters in the back, today's choice a robust timepiece with intricate detailing. "Today, we'll chart the course for AI implementation and adoption in project management."

The first step to any journey is preparation," Phill began, guiding his students through an analysis of organizational readiness.

"Adopting AI isn't as simple as flipping a switch; it requires planning, resource allocation, and a culture ready to embrace change."

12.1 Assessing Organizational Readiness for AI Adoption

In this chapter, we explore the importance of assessing organizational readiness for AI adoption and the factors that influence successful implementation. Adopting AI technologies requires careful evaluation of an organization's capabilities, resources, and cultural readiness to embrace and leverage AI effectively.

We discuss the key considerations for assessing organizational readiness, including technological infrastructure, data quality and availability, workforce skills, and leadership support. Understanding these factors helps organizations identify potential gaps and challenges that need to be addressed before implementing AI. We emphasize the significance of conducting a thorough assessment to ensure that the organization is prepared to leverage AI's full potential.

Before implementing AI, it is important to assess the organization's readiness for AI adoption. This includes assessing the organization's culture, data, and technical capabilities.

- Organizational culture: AI adoption is more likely to be successful in organizations that are open to change and innovation. Organizations that are risk-averse or have a siloed culture may be less likely to be successful with AI adoption.

- Data: AI models require data to train and operate. Organizations that have access to large amounts of high-quality data will be more successful with AI adoption.

- Technical capabilities: AI models require technical expertise to develop and deploy. Organizations that have the necessary technical capabilities will be more successful with AI adoption.

Armed with an understanding of readiness, Phill navigated the class through the creation of an AI implementation roadmap. "A clear plan paves the way for smooth implementation, minimizing disruptions and maximizing benefits."

12.2 Developing an AI Implementation Roadmap

Next, we will review the process of developing an AI implementation roadmap. An AI implementation roadmap serves as a strategic plan that outlines the steps, milestones, and timelines for adopting and integrating AI into an organization's operations. It provides a clear direction for AI implementation, ensuring a systematic and structured approach.

Some key components of an AI implementation roadmap, include defining goals and objectives, identifying AI use cases, assessing resource requirements, and planning for data acquisition and integration. It is important to align the roadmap with the organization's overall strategic objectives and involving key stakeholders in the planning process. By developing a well-defined implementation roadmap, organizations can navigate the complexities of AI adoption and ensure a smooth transition.

Once the organization has been assessed for readiness, an AI implementation roadmap can be developed. The roadmap should include the following:

- Goals: The goals of the AI implementation should be clearly defined.

- Timeline: The timeline for the AI implementation should be realistic and achievable.

- Resources: The resources required for the AI implementation should be identified.

- Metrics: The metrics for success of the AI implementation should be defined.

Phill then shifted gears, focusing on the human side of AI adoption. "Resistance to change is natural," he explained, "but it can be overcome with the right strategies." He shared insights on change management, stakeholder engagement, and the power of transparent communication.

12.3 Overcoming Resistance and Ensuring Successful AI Integration

In this section, we address the challenges associated with overcoming resistance to AI adoption and ensuring successful integration within the organization. Resistance to change is a common barrier to AI implementation, and organizations need to proactively manage this resistance to foster a culture of acceptance and embrace new technologies.
We discuss strategies for overcoming resistance, such as effective change management, clear communication, and fostering a culture of learning and experimentation. We emphasize the importance of addressing concerns related to job displacement, data privacy, and ethical considerations. Successful AI integration requires creating a supportive environment that encourages collaboration, continuous learning, and the exploration of AI opportunities.

There may be some resistance to AI adoption within the organization. This resistance can be overcome by communicating the benefits of AI to employees and by providing them with training on how to use AI.

It is also important to ensure that AI is integrated into the organization's culture and processes. This can be done by involving employees in the development and deployment of AI models and by making sure that AI is used in a way that is consistent with the organization's values.

As is tradition," Phill concluded with a chuckle, "we end with an exercise. Today, you'll craft an AI adoption plan for a hypothetical organization. Remember to consider readiness, roadmap, and resistance in your plan."

With that, Phill sat back, observing as jesters and scholars alike got to work. The hum of the projector served as a comforting backdrop to the murmur of collaborative discussions and the flurry of ideas that filled the room, marking another successful day in their exploration of AI in project management.

12.4 Exercise: Developing an AI Adoption Plan

Assignment: Developing a Comprehensive AI Adoption Plan

Objective: To develop a comprehensive plan for implementing AI within a specific organizational context. Participants should first choose an organization for this assignment. Then take into account the organization's readiness, goals, and challenges, and propose strategies to address them.

Instructions:

1. **Understanding the Context**: Analyze your selected organization, its industry, its readiness for AI, and its main goals and challenges. Understand the unique needs and requirements of the organization. The goals of the AI implementation should be clearly defined.

2. **Identifying Potential Benefits and Risks**: Identify potential benefits of AI adoption for the organization, as well as potential risks. Consider both short-term and long-term impacts.

3. **Developing an AI Adoption Plan**: Develop a comprehensive plan for implementing AI in the organization. This should include:

   - Key milestones: Outline the major stages of AI adoption, from initial planning to implementation and review.

   - Resource allocation strategies: Detail how resources (including time, personnel, and funding) should be allocated at each stage of AI adoption.

   - Change management considerations: Discuss how the organization can prepare its employees for AI adoption and manage changes effectively.

   - Resistance: How will you overcome resistance to AI adoption within the organization?

   - Integration: How will you ensure that AI is integrated into the organization's culture and processes?

4. **Overcoming Challenges**: Propose strategies to overcome potential challenges in AI adoption. This could include technical challenges, employee resistance, or data privacy concerns.

5. **Submission**: Submit your AI adoption plan in a structured format. It should be clear, concise, and demonstrate a comprehensive understanding of AI adoption in an organizational context.

Expected Outcome:

By completing this assignment, participants will gain practical insights into the process of developing an AI adoption plan. They will learn how to analyze an organization's readiness for AI, identify potential benefits and risks of AI adoption, and develop strategies for overcoming challenges and ensuring successful AI integration. The assignment will help participants understand the complexities of AI adoption in an organizational context and prepare them for real-world AI implementation challenges.

CHAPTER THIRTEEN: AI FUTURE TRENDS IN PROJECT MANAGEMENT

> **"**
>
> *The future of project management is undoubtedly intertwined with the intelligent and strategic use of AI.*

Phill adjusted his tie, its bright colors matching the excitement in his eyes. "Class, we're about to embark on a journey that goes beyond what we've learned so far. Let's explore the impact of emerging technologies on project management."

The familiar warm tone of Peter Baker's voice filled the room announcing. "In this chapter, we explore the impact of emerging technologies on project management and how they intersect with artificial intelligence (AI). As technology continues to evolve rapidly, project managers need to stay abreast of these trends to effectively adapt and leverage new opportunities."

"We discuss various emerging technologies, such as Internet of Things (IoT), blockchain, augmented reality (AR), and virtual reality (VR), and their potential impact on project management practices. We examine how these technologies can enhance data collection, collaboration, communication, and decision-making processes. Furthermore, we explore how AI can be integrated with these emerging technologies to create synergistic effects and drive innovation in project management." The slide deck advanced to 13.1.

13.1 Emerging Technologies and their Impact on Project Management

There are a number of emerging technologies that are likely to have a significant impact on project management in the future. These technologies include:

- Artificial intelligence (AI): AI is already being used to automate tasks in project management, such as scheduling, budgeting, and risk management. In the future, AI is likely to be used to even more complex tasks, such as project planning and decision-making.

- Big data: Big data is the collection of large and complex datasets. Big data can be used to gain insights into project performance and to identify trends that can be used to improve project management practices.

- Blockchain: Blockchain is a distributed ledger technology that can be used to track and manage project data. Blockchain has the potential to improve the transparency and efficiency of project management.

- Virtual reality (VR) and augmented reality (AR)**: VR and AR can be used to create immersive experiences that can be used to train project managers and to simulate project environments.

Then, the troublemaker of the class, Joey, quipped, "So, will quantum computers do all our work while we sip margaritas on the beach?" The class erupted in laughter, but Phil merely grinned. "Why not, Joey? If it can enhance efficiency and accuracy, why shouldn't we embrace it? But remember, technology aids us; it doesn't replace us."

Moving on to the next segment, Phill spoke about how AI-driven automation and robotics are changing the dynamics of project management. "From automated reporting to robotic process automation, AI is redefining traditional roles in project management," Phill explained. Amidst the chatter of awe and speculation, even the jesters in the class seemed to understand the transformative potential of AI.

13.2 AI-Driven Automation and Robotics

Next, we go into the realm of AI-driven automation and robotics and their implications for project management. Automation technologies powered by AI can significantly impact project execution by automating repetitive and time-consuming tasks, increasing efficiency, and improving overall productivity.

AI-driven automation and robotics can streamline project workflows, enhance resource allocation, and enable more accurate and faster data processing. There are potential benefits and challenges associated with the integration of automation technologies, including considerations such as job displacement and workforce reskilling. Understanding the capabilities and limitations of AI-driven automation and robotics is crucial for project managers to effectively harness their potential.

AI-driven automation and robotics are already being used in project management. For example, AI-powered chatbots can be used to answer project-related questions, and robots can be used to automate tasks such as data entry and testing.

In the future, AI-driven automation and robotics are likely to be used to even more complex tasks. For example, AI-powered robots could be used to manage project resources, and AI-powered chatbots could be used to provide real-time project support.

13.3 Ethical and Social Implications of AI in Project Management

In this section, we address the ethical and social implications of AI in project management. As AI technologies become more prevalent, it is essential to consider the potential impact on privacy, bias, fairness, and human-machine collaboration.

As Phill transitioned to the ethical considerations, the room fell quiet. He discussed how AI's implications extend beyond practical applications, delving into the ethical and social aspects. "Remember," Phill emphasized, "while AI offers numerous benefits, it's crucial to consider data privacy, job displacement, and the potential for misuse."

The use of AI in project management raises a number of ethical and social implications. For example, it is important to ensure that AI is used in a way that is fair and unbiased. It is also important to consider the impact of AI on the workforce, as AI could lead to job losses in some areas. The world of AI is ever-evolving, and as project managers, we need to stay ahead of the curve. But it's not just about staying informed on the latest developments - we also need to deeply consider the ethical and social implications of AI integration. By doing so, we can leverage AI in a responsible and impactful way, paving the road for innovation, efficiency, and success in project management.

It is important to have a discussion about the ethical and social implications of AI in project management. This discussion should involve project managers, stakeholders, and the wider community.

Conclusion

The future of AI in project management is full of possibilities. AI has the potential to revolutionize project management, making it more efficient, effective, and transparent. However, it is important to consider the ethical and social implications of AI in project management. By having a discussion about these implications, we can ensure that AI is used in a way that benefits society as a whole.

As he finished his presentation, Phill noticed a change in the room. The jesters weren't jesting, and the serious students seemed lost in thought. He realized that this journey through AI in project management had not only equipped them with technical knowledge but also instilled in them a sense of responsibility towards its ethical use. As the projector hummed in the background, Phill knew that this journey was just the beginning for these future project managers.

The exercise in this chapter provides an opportunity to think about the future of AI in project management. By completing this exercise, you will gain a better understanding of ethics in AI and the potential impact of AI on project management.

13.4 Exercise: Envisioning the Future of AI in Project Management

Ready to put your forward-thinking cap on? In this exercise, you're going to envision what the future holds for AI in project management. To help you dive in, here are a few prompts:

1. Imagine the tasks that could be automated by AI in the future.
2. Contemplate how AI might transform the way we manage projects.
3. Think deeply about the potential ethical and social implications that come with integrating AI into project management.

Your task? Weave your thoughts into a brief essay, outlining your vision of the future of AI in project management.

This exercise is designed to ignite your creativity, provoke critical thinking about ethical AI practices, and give you a taste of what's to come in the realm of AI-enhanced project management.

Happy brainstorming, and remember - the future of AI in project management is as exciting as we make it!"

CHAPTER FOURTEEN: CONCLUSION AND KEY TAKEAWAYS

> **"**
>
> *As project managers, we are at the helm of this AI-driven revolution, navigating towards unprecedented efficiencies, insights, and successes.*

With a fond smile, Phill straightened his vibrant tie, a small signal to his class that their time together was drawing to an end. His watch, a classic piece from his collection, marked the bittersweet passage of time.

"Ladies and gentlemen, jesters and scholars," he began, "we've reached our last chapter. Today, we recap, reflect, and put all we've learned into action."

"The AI landscape is vast and complex, but its potential in project management is unarguable," he started. He took the class on a journey through the topics they had covered, highlighting the role of AI in predictive, agile, and hybrid project management.

14.1 Recap of AI's Role in Project Management

In this final chapter, we recap the role of artificial intelligence (AI) in project management and summarize the key concepts discussed throughout the book. AI has emerged as a powerful tool that can augment project management practices, improve decision-making, enhance efficiency, and drive project success.

We revisit the various ways in which AI can be integrated into project management, including its applications in hybrid project management approaches, Scrum practices, Kanban practices, data analytics, risk analysis, performance tracking, and more. We emphasize that AI is not meant to replace human project managers but rather to enhance their capabilities and provide valuable insights.

Artificial intelligence (AI) has the potential to revolutionize project management. AI can be used to automate tasks, improve decision-making, and gain insights into project performance.

Here are some of the ways that AI is being used in project management today:

- Automating tasks: AI can be used to automate tasks such as scheduling, budgeting, and risk management. This frees up project managers to focus on more strategic tasks.

- Improving decision-making: AI can be used to analyze data and make predictions. This information can be used to help project managers make better decisions about project planning, execution, and risk management.

- Gaining insights: AI can be used to gain insights into project performance. This information can be used to identify trends and patterns that can be used to improve project management practices.

Next, Phill turned to the lessons they had collectively unearthed. "AI is not just a tool; it's a powerful ally that can help us navigate the intricate terrain of project management. But remember," he said, his gaze sweeping across the room, "it's not a substitute for human intuition and creativity."

14.2 Key Lessons Learned

Next, we highlight the key lessons learned from exploring the integration of AI in project management. These lessons serve as valuable takeaways for project managers and organizations considering the adoption of AI in their projects:

1. Understand project characteristics and stakeholder expectations to determine the most suitable AI integration approach.

2. Recognize the strengths and limitations of different project management methodologies and leverage AI to create hybrid approaches that align with project requirements.

3. Leverage AI in planning and estimation, risk analysis, performance tracking, and decision-making processes to enhance project outcomes.

4. Overcome resistance to AI adoption through effective change management, clear communication, and fostering a supportive culture.

5. Consider the ethical and social implications of AI and ensure responsible AI practices are followed.

By reflecting on these key lessons, project managers can better navigate the integration of AI into their projects and maximize the benefits it offers.

Here are some of the key lessons that we have learned about AI in project management:

- AI is a powerful tool that can be used to improve project management.

- AI is not a replacement for project managers. AI can be used to automate tasks and improve decision-making, but it is still important for project managers to be involved in the project planning and execution process.

- The use of AI in project management raises ethical and social implications. It is important to have a discussion about these implications and to ensure that AI is used in a way that benefits society as a whole.

"As a final exercise, and perhaps the most crucial one," Phill announced, "you'll apply the AI concepts we've discussed to a real-world project scenario. Show me how you'd leverage AI to enhance project management practices."

Phill's final words rang out in the classroom, leaving a silence filled with nostalgia. The projector hummed its final tune as the class disbanded, each student carrying with them a wealth of knowledge, insightful experiences, and a newfound respect for AI in project management.

14.3 Final Exercise: Applying AI Concepts to a Real-world Project

Objective: This exercise is designed to test your understanding of AI concepts and principles discussed throughout the book, applying them to a real-world project scenario.

Scenario: You have recently been assigned as the project manager for a city's smart infrastructure project. The project aims to integrate IoT-enabled devices across the city's public infrastructure to improve efficiency and responsiveness.

Instructions:

1. Identify AI Opportunities: Review the project scenario and identify at least three areas where AI could be integrated to improve project management outcomes. Justify your choices by explaining how AI could enhance these aspects.

2. AI Concepts and Solutions: Based on your identified opportunities, propose specific AI-driven solutions for each one. Discuss how these solutions would work and how they could benefit the project. AI concepts could include machine learning, natural language processing, computer vision, etc.

3. Stakeholder Management: Given the unique requirements, challenges, and stakeholders' expectations of this project, discuss how you plan to manage these aspects while implementing AI solutions.

4. Ethics and Social Consideration: What ethical and social implications might arise from integrating AI into this project? How would you propose to address these considerations?

5. Deliverable: Prepare a detailed report outlining your answers. This report should be at least 5 pages long and include your rationale for each AI integration, a thorough explanation of how the chosen AI concepts would work, and an outline of potential ethical and social implications.

By completing this final exercise, you will consolidate your understanding of AI's role in project management, effectively identifying AI opportunities and devising strategies for AI implementation in real-world project scenarios. This exercise reflects the ongoing nature of learning in the field of AI and project management, emphasizing the importance of continuous growth and adaptation in this rapidly evolving landscape.

Conclusion

This book has explored the role of AI in project management. We have learned that AI is a powerful tool that can be used to improve project management. However, it is important to use AI in a responsible way and to consider the ethical and social implications.

Only those project managers who are daring and insightful enough to embrace AI today will ride the waves of the future successfully. A single word should suffice for the prudent: AI is not a fleeting trend; it's here for the long haul.

Over the years, AI has evolved and transformed, and now it's prominently within our horizon. To disregard it or deny its existence, or to find reasons not to leverage it ethically and judiciously in our profession, would be unwise.

I urge you to treat this as a starting point to ascend to new heights by embracing AI's power ethically and intentionally, to better serve your stakeholders and your company, and ultimately deliver superior outcomes.

All the best in your journey ahead!

Your Friend Phill

Appendix: Resources and Tools

A.1 Recommended Books and Research Papers

1. 5 Implications of Artificial Intelligence for Project Management

   https://www.pmi.org/learning/publications/pm-network/digital-exclusives/implications-of-ai

2. Real Advantage: PMI's Latest Pulse of the Profession® Report Reveals the Power of AI (2019)

   https://www.pmi.org/learning/publications/pm-network/digital-exclusives/implications-of-ai

3. Hosley, W. N. (1987). The application of artificial intelligence software to project management. *Project Management Journal, 18*(3), 73–75.

   https://www.pmi.org/learning/library/application-artificial-intelligence-software-pm-5234

A.2 Online Learning Platforms and Courses

4. ChatGPT & Artificial Intelligence (AI) for Project Managers

   https://www.udemy.com/chatgpts

About the Author

Phill C. Akinwale, PMP, is a highly experienced project management professional with a proven track record in both government and private sectors. Throughout his career, he has worked with renowned companies such as Motorola, Honeywell, Emerson, Skillsoft, Citigroup, Iron Mountain, Brown and Caldwell, US Airways, and CVS Caremark, managing operational endeavors, projects, and project controls.

With his extensive knowledge and expertise in various facets of Project Management, Phill has become a trusted figure in the field. He has trained project management professionals worldwide, including prestigious organizations like NASA, FBI, USAF, USACE, US Army, and the Department of Transport. Over the past 15 years, he has provided training across five editions of the PMBOK® Guide, showcasing his commitment to staying up-to-date with industry standards.

Phill holds an impressive twelve project management certifications, with a notable focus on Agile Project Management. His certifications include Certified ScrumMaster (CSM), PMI Agile Certified Practitioner (PMI-ACP), Professional Scrum Master (PSM), Professional Scrum Product Owner (PSPO), Professional Agile Leadership (PAL), and Scaled Professional Scrum (SPS). This diverse range of certifications reflects his dedication to mastering various project management methodologies.

In addition to his project management expertise, Phill is a certified coach and speaker through the John Maxwell team. Leveraging his leadership and soft skills, he delivers impactful workshops, seminars, keynote speeches, and coaching sessions. He is passionate about guiding individuals, teams, and organizations in their desired direction, equipping them with the tools and knowledge to achieve their goals.

Phill is also a prolific author, having written over 20 books on a diverse range of topics. His written works cover areas such as bullying (including "The Bird Brained Bullies"), leadership, conflict resolution, time travel ("The Time Machine Project"), and even comics ("Project VBX 11"). Furthermore, he has created two short movies that explore themes of leadership drama in the workplace and project management.

With his vast experience, certifications, and passion for guiding others, Phill C. Akinwale, PMP, is a valuable asset to any organization or individual seeking project management expertise, leadership development, and personal growth.

www.ingramcontent.com/pod-product-compliance
Lightning Source LLC
LaVergne TN
LVHW060142070326
832902LV00018B/2909